C-608  CAREER EXAMINATION SERIES

*This is your PASSBOOK for...*

# Power Maintainer- Group B

*Test Preparation Study Guide
Questions & Answers*

# COPYRIGHT NOTICE

This book is SOLELY intended for, is sold ONLY to, and its use is RESTRICTED to individual, bona fide applicants or candidates who qualify by virtue of having seriously filed applications for appropriate license, certificate, professional and/or promotional advancement, higher school matriculation, scholarship, or other legitimate requirements of education and/or governmental authorities.

This book is NOT intended for use, class instruction, tutoring, training, duplication, copying, reprinting, excerption, or adaptation, etc., by:

1) Other publishers
2) Proprietors and/or Instructors of "Coaching" and/or Preparatory Courses
3) Personnel and/or Training Divisions of commercial, industrial, and governmental organizations
4) Schools, colleges, or universities and/or their departments and staffs, including teachers and other personnel
5) Testing Agencies or Bureaus
6) Study groups which seek by the purchase of a single volume to copy and/or duplicate and/or adapt this material for use by the group as a whole without having purchased individual volumes for each of the members of the group
7) Et al.

Such persons would be in violation of appropriate Federal and State statutes.

PROVISION OF LICENSING AGREEMENTS – Recognized educational, commercial, industrial, and governmental institutions and organizations, and others legitimately engaged in educational pursuits, including training, testing, and measurement activities, may address request for a licensing agreement to the copyright owners, who will determine whether, and under what conditions, including fees and charges, the materials in this book may be used them.  In other words, a licensing facility exists for the legitimate use of the material in this book on other than an individual basis.  However, it is asseverated and affirmed here that the material in this book CANNOT be used without the receipt of the express permission of such a licensing agreement from the Publishers.  Inquiries re licensing should be addressed to the company, attention rights and permissions department.

All rights reserved, including the right of reproduction in whole or in part, in any form or by any means, electronic or mechanical, including photocopying, recording, or by any information storage and retrieval system, without permission in writing from the Publisher.

Copyright © 2025 by
## National Learning Corporation

212 Michael Drive, Syosset, NY 11791
(516) 921-8888 • www.passbooks.com
E-mail: info@passbooks.com

# PASSBOOK® SERIES

THE *PASSBOOK® SERIES* has been created to prepare applicants and candidates for the ultimate academic battlefield – the examination room.

At some time in our lives, each and every one of us may be required to take an examination – for validation, matriculation, admission, qualification, registration, certification, or licensure.

Based on the assumption that every applicant or candidate has met the basic formal educational standards, has taken the required number of courses, and read the necessary texts, the *PASSBOOK® SERIES* furnishes the one special preparation which may assure passing with confidence, instead of failing with insecurity. Examination questions – together with answers – are furnished as the basic vehicle for study so that the mysteries of the examination and its compounding difficulties may be eliminated or diminished by a sure method.

This book is meant to help you pass your examination provided that you qualify and are serious in your objective.

The entire field is reviewed through the huge store of content information which is succinctly presented through a provocative and challenging approach – the question-and-answer method.

A climate of success is established by furnishing the correct answers at the end of each test.

You soon learn to recognize types of questions, forms of questions, and patterns of questioning. You may even begin to anticipate expected outcomes.

You perceive that many questions are repeated or adapted so that you can gain acute insights, which may enable you to score many sure points.

You learn how to confront new questions, or types of questions, and to attack them confidently and work out the correct answers.

You note objectives and emphases, and recognize pitfalls and dangers, so that you may make positive educational adjustments.

Moreover, you are kept fully informed in relation to new concepts, methods, practices, and directions in the field.

You discover that you are actually taking the examination all the time: you are preparing for the examination by "taking" an examination, not by reading extraneous and/or supererogatory textbooks.

In short, this PASSBOOK®, used directedly, should be an important factor in helping you to pass your test.

# POWER MAINTAINER-GROUP B

## DUTIES AND RESPONSIBILITIES
Operates, maintains installs, inspects, tests, alters, and repairs the substation equipment and associated supervisory control equipment. Performs such other duties as the authority is authorized by law to prescribe in its regulations.

## EXAMPLES OF TYPICAL TASKS
Operates, maintains, services, and repairs various types of power substation equipment and their associated controls, including: mercury arc and silicon rectifiers, rotary converters, high tension and low tension switch gear, automatic relay panels and circuits, auxiliary equipment and accessories. Sectionalizes power equipment. If assigned, performs inspection work on new equipment and material at manufacturing plants. Makes computations. Keeps records. Writes reports.

## SUBJECT OF EXAMINATION
The written test will be of the multiple-choice type and may include questions on the :
1. Technical operation, maintenance, repair, and testing of electrical power equipment used to supply power, including rectifiers, rotary converters, motors, generators, and associated auxiliary and control equipment;
2. Rules and regulations and safety procedures applicable to the power division;
3. Operation of electrical test equipment; and
4. Fundamental electrical circuits and electrical equipment.

# HOW TO TAKE A TEST

## I. YOU MUST PASS AN EXAMINATION

### A. WHAT EVERY CANDIDATE SHOULD KNOW

Examination applicants often ask us for help in preparing for the written test. What can I study in advance? What kinds of questions will be asked? How will the test be given? How will the papers be graded?

As an applicant for a civil service examination, you may be wondering about some of these things. Our purpose here is to suggest effective methods of advance study and to describe civil service examinations.

Your chances for success on this examination can be increased if you know how to prepare. Those "pre-examination jitters" can be reduced if you know what to expect. You can even experience an adventure in good citizenship if you know why civil service exams are given.

### B. WHY ARE CIVIL SERVICE EXAMINATIONS GIVEN?

Civil service examinations are important to you in two ways. As a citizen, you want public jobs filled by employees who know how to do their work. As a job seeker, you want a fair chance to compete for that job on an equal footing with other candidates. The best-known means of accomplishing this two-fold goal is the competitive examination.

Exams are widely publicized throughout the nation. They may be administered for jobs in federal, state, city, municipal, town or village governments or agencies.

Any citizen may apply, with some limitations, such as the age or residence of applicants. Your experience and education may be reviewed to see whether you meet the requirements for the particular examination. When these requirements exist, they are reasonable and applied consistently to all applicants. Thus, a competitive examination may cause you some uneasiness now, but it is your privilege and safeguard.

### C. HOW ARE CIVIL SERVICE EXAMS DEVELOPED?

Examinations are carefully written by trained technicians who are specialists in the field known as "psychological measurement," in consultation with recognized authorities in the field of work that the test will cover. These experts recommend the subject matter areas or skills to be tested; only those knowledges or skills important to your success on the job are included. The most reliable books and source materials available are used as references. Together, the experts and technicians judge the difficulty level of the questions.

Test technicians know how to phrase questions so that the problem is clearly stated. Their ethics do not permit "trick" or "catch" questions. Questions may have been tried out on sample groups, or subjected to statistical analysis, to determine their usefulness.

Written tests are often used in combination with performance tests, ratings of training and experience, and oral interviews. All of these measures combine to form the best-known means of finding the right person for the right job.

## II. HOW TO PASS THE WRITTEN TEST

### A. NATURE OF THE EXAMINATION

To prepare intelligently for civil service examinations, you should know how they differ from school examinations you have taken. In school you were assigned certain definite pages to read or subjects to cover. The examination questions were quite detailed and usually emphasized memory. Civil service exams, on the other hand, try to discover your present ability to perform the duties of a position, plus your potentiality to learn these duties. In other words, a civil service exam attempts to predict how successful you will be. Questions cover such a broad area that they cannot be as minute and detailed as school exam questions.

In the public service similar kinds of work, or positions, are grouped together in one "class." This process is known as *position-classification*. All the positions in a class are paid according to the salary range for that class. One class title covers all of these positions, and they are all tested by the same examination.

### B. FOUR BASIC STEPS

#### 1) Study the announcement

How, then, can you know what subjects to study? Our best answer is: "Learn as much as possible about the class of positions for which you've applied." The exam will test the knowledge, skills and abilities needed to do the work.

Your most valuable source of information about the position you want is the official exam announcement. This announcement lists the training and experience qualifications. Check these standards and apply only if you come reasonably close to meeting them.

The brief description of the position in the examination announcement offers some clues to the subjects which will be tested. Think about the job itself. Review the duties in your mind. Can you perform them, or are there some in which you are rusty? Fill in the blank spots in your preparation.

Many jurisdictions preview the written test in the exam announcement by including a section called "Knowledge and Abilities Required," "Scope of the Examination," or some similar heading. Here you will find out specifically what fields will be tested.

#### 2) Review your own background

Once you learn in general what the position is all about, and what you need to know to do the work, ask yourself which subjects you already know fairly well and which need improvement. You may wonder whether to concentrate on improving your strong areas or on building some background in your fields of weakness. When the announcement has specified "some knowledge" or "considerable knowledge," or has used adjectives like "beginning principles of..." or "advanced ... methods," you can get a clue as to the number and difficulty of questions to be asked in any given field. More questions, and hence broader coverage, would be included for those subjects which are more important in the work. Now weigh your strengths and weaknesses against the job requirements and prepare accordingly.

#### 3) Determine the level of the position

Another way to tell how intensively you should prepare is to understand the level of the job for which you are applying. Is it the entering level? In other words, is this the position in which beginners in a field of work are hired? Or is it an intermediate or advanced level? Sometimes this is indicated by such words as "Junior" or "Senior" in the class title. Other jurisdictions use Roman numerals to designate the level – Clerk I, Clerk II, for example. The word "Supervisor" sometimes appears in the title. If the level is not indicated by the title, check the description of duties. Will you be working under very close supervision, or will you have responsibility for independent decisions in this work?

### 4) Choose appropriate study materials

Now that you know the subjects to be examined and the relative amount of each subject to be covered, you can choose suitable study materials. For beginning level jobs, or even advanced ones, if you have a pronounced weakness in some aspect of your training, read a modern, standard textbook in that field. Be sure it is up to date and has general coverage. Such books are normally available at your library, and the librarian will be glad to help you locate one. For entry-level positions, questions of appropriate difficulty are chosen – neither highly advanced questions, nor those too simple. Such questions require careful thought but not advanced training.

If the position for which you are applying is technical or advanced, you will read more advanced, specialized material. If you are already familiar with the basic principles of your field, elementary textbooks would waste your time. Concentrate on advanced textbooks and technical periodicals. Think through the concepts and review difficult problems in your field.

These are all general sources. You can get more ideas on your own initiative, following these leads. For example, training manuals and publications of the government agency which employs workers in your field can be useful, particularly for technical and professional positions. A letter or visit to the government department involved may result in more specific study suggestions, and certainly will provide you with a more definite idea of the exact nature of the position you are seeking.

## III. KINDS OF TESTS

Tests are used for purposes other than measuring knowledge and ability to perform specified duties. For some positions, it is equally important to test ability to make adjustments to new situations or to profit from training. In others, basic mental abilities not dependent on information are essential. Questions which test these things may not appear as pertinent to the duties of the position as those which test for knowledge and information. Yet they are often highly important parts of a fair examination. For very general questions, it is almost impossible to help you direct your study efforts. What we can do is to point out some of the more common of these general abilities needed in public service positions and describe some typical questions.

1) General information

Broad, general information has been found useful for predicting job success in some kinds of work. This is tested in a variety of ways, from vocabulary lists to questions about current events. Basic background in some field of work, such as sociology or economics, may be sampled in a group of questions. Often these are principles which have become familiar to most persons through exposure rather than through formal training. It is difficult to advise you how to study for these questions; being alert to the world around you is our best suggestion.

2) Verbal ability

An example of an ability needed in many positions is verbal or language ability. Verbal ability is, in brief, the ability to use and understand words. Vocabulary and grammar tests are typical measures of this ability. Reading comprehension or paragraph interpretation questions are common in many kinds of civil service tests. You are given a paragraph of written material and asked to find its central meaning.

3) Numerical ability

Number skills can be tested by the familiar arithmetic problem, by checking paired lists of numbers to see which are alike and which are different, or by interpreting charts and graphs. In the latter test, a graph may be printed in the test booklet which you are asked to use as the basis for answering questions.

4) Observation

A popular test for law-enforcement positions is the observation test. A picture is shown to you for several minutes, then taken away. Questions about the picture test your ability to observe both details and larger elements.

5) Following directions

In many positions in the public service, the employee must be able to carry out written instructions dependably and accurately. You may be given a chart with several columns, each column listing a variety of information. The questions require you to carry out directions involving the information given in the chart.

6) Skills and aptitudes

Performance tests effectively measure some manual skills and aptitudes. When the skill is one in which you are trained, such as typing or shorthand, you can practice. These tests are often very much like those given in business school or high school courses. For many of the other skills and aptitudes, however, no short-time preparation can be made. Skills and abilities natural to you or that you have developed throughout your lifetime are being tested.

Many of the general questions just described provide all the data needed to answer the questions and ask you to use your reasoning ability to find the answers. Your best preparation for these tests, as well as for tests of facts and ideas, is to be at your physical and mental best. You, no doubt, have your own methods of getting into an exam-taking mood and keeping "in shape." The next section lists some ideas on this subject.


IV. KINDS OF QUESTIONS

Only rarely is the "essay" question, which you answer in narrative form, used in civil service tests. Civil service tests are usually of the short-answer type. Full instructions for answering these questions will be given to you at the examination. But in case this is your first experience with short-answer questions and separate answer sheets, here is what you need to know:

**1) Multiple-choice Questions**

Most popular of the short-answer questions is the "multiple choice" or "best answer" question. It can be used, for example, to test for factual knowledge, ability to solve problems or judgment in meeting situations found at work.

A multiple-choice question is normally one of three types—
- It can begin with an incomplete statement followed by several possible endings. You are to find the one ending which *best* completes the statement, although some of the others may not be entirely wrong.
- It can also be a complete statement in the form of a question which is answered by choosing one of the statements listed.

- It can be in the form of a problem – again you select the best answer.

Here is an example of a multiple-choice question with a discussion which should give you some clues as to the method for choosing the right answer:

When an employee has a complaint about his assignment, the action which will *best* help him overcome his difficulty is to
   A. discuss his difficulty with his coworkers
   B. take the problem to the head of the organization
   C. take the problem to the person who gave him the assignment
   D. say nothing to anyone about his complaint

In answering this question, you should study each of the choices to find which is best. Consider choice "A" – Certainly an employee may discuss his complaint with fellow employees, but no change or improvement can result, and the complaint remains unresolved. Choice "B" is a poor choice since the head of the organization probably does not know what assignment you have been given, and taking your problem to him is known as "going over the head" of the supervisor. The supervisor, or person who made the assignment, is the person who can clarify it or correct any injustice. Choice "C" is, therefore, correct. To say nothing, as in choice "D," is unwise. Supervisors have and interest in knowing the problems employees are facing, and the employee is seeking a solution to his problem.

## 2) True/False Questions

The "true/false" or "right/wrong" form of question is sometimes used. Here a complete statement is given. Your job is to decide whether the statement is right or wrong.

SAMPLE: A roaming cell-phone call to a nearby city costs less than a non-roaming call to a distant city.

This statement is wrong, or false, since roaming calls are more expensive.

This is not a complete list of all possible question forms, although most of the others are variations of these common types. You will always get complete directions for answering questions. Be sure you understand *how* to mark your answers – ask questions until you do.

## V. RECORDING YOUR ANSWERS

Computer terminals are used more and more today for many different kinds of exams.

For an examination with very few applicants, you may be told to record your answers in the test booklet itself. Separate answer sheets are much more common. If this separate answer sheet is to be scored by machine – and this is often the case – it is highly important that you mark your answers correctly in order to get credit.

An electronic scoring machine is often used in civil service offices because of the speed with which papers can be scored. Machine-scored answer sheets must be marked with a pencil, which will be given to you. This pencil has a high graphite content which responds to the electronic scoring machine. As a matter of fact, stray dots may register as answers, so do not let your pencil rest on the answer sheet while you are pondering the correct answer. Also, if your pencil lead breaks or is otherwise defective, ask for another.

Since the answer sheet will be dropped in a slot in the scoring machine, be careful not to bend the corners or get the paper crumpled.

The answer sheet normally has five vertical columns of numbers, with 30 numbers to a column. These numbers correspond to the question numbers in your test booklet. After each number, going across the page are four or five pairs of dotted lines. These short dotted lines have small letters or numbers above them. The first two pairs may also have a "T" or "F" above the letters. This indicates that the first two pairs only are to be used if the questions are of the true-false type. If the questions are multiple choice, disregard the "T" and "F" and pay attention only to the small letters or numbers.

Answer your questions in the manner of the sample that follows:

32. The largest city in the United States is
    A. Washington, D.C.
    B. New York City
    C. Chicago
    D. Detroit
    E. San Francisco

1) Choose the answer you think is best. (New York City is the largest, so "B" is correct.)
2) Find the row of dotted lines numbered the same as the question you are answering. (Find row number 32)
3) Find the pair of dotted lines corresponding to the answer. (Find the pair of lines under the mark "B.")
4) Make a solid black mark between the dotted lines.


## VI. BEFORE THE TEST

Common sense will help you find procedures to follow to get ready for an examination. Too many of us, however, overlook these sensible measures. Indeed, nervousness and fatigue have been found to be the most serious reasons why applicants fail to do their best on civil service tests. Here is a list of reminders:

- Begin your preparation early – Don't wait until the last minute to go scurrying around for books and materials or to find out what the position is all about.
- Prepare continuously – An hour a night for a week is better than an all-night cram session. This has been definitely established. What is more, a night a week for a month will return better dividends than crowding your study into a shorter period of time.
- Locate the place of the exam – You have been sent a notice telling you when and where to report for the examination. If the location is in a different town or otherwise unfamiliar to you, it would be well to inquire the best route and learn something about the building.
- Relax the night before the test – Allow your mind to rest. Do not study at all that night. Plan some mild recreation or diversion; then go to bed early and get a good night's sleep.
- Get up early enough to make a leisurely trip to the place for the test – This way unforeseen events, traffic snarls, unfamiliar buildings, etc. will not upset you.
- Dress comfortably – A written test is not a fashion show. You will be known by number and not by name, so wear something comfortable.

- Leave excess paraphernalia at home – Shopping bags and odd bundles will get in your way. You need bring only the items mentioned in the official notice you received; usually everything you need is provided. Do not bring reference books to the exam. They will only confuse those last minutes and be taken away from you when in the test room.
- Arrive somewhat ahead of time – If because of transportation schedules you must get there very early, bring a newspaper or magazine to take your mind off yourself while waiting.
- Locate the examination room – When you have found the proper room, you will be directed to the seat or part of the room where you will sit. Sometimes you are given a sheet of instructions to read while you are waiting. Do not fill out any forms until you are told to do so; just read them and be prepared.
- Relax and prepare to listen to the instructions
- If you have any physical problem that may keep you from doing your best, be sure to tell the test administrator. If you are sick or in poor health, you really cannot do your best on the exam. You can come back and take the test some other time.

## VII. AT THE TEST

The day of the test is here and you have the test booklet in your hand. The temptation to get going is very strong. Caution! There is more to success than knowing the right answers. You must know how to identify your papers and understand variations in the type of short-answer question used in this particular examination. Follow these suggestions for maximum results from your efforts:

### 1) Cooperate with the monitor

The test administrator has a duty to create a situation in which you can be as much at ease as possible. He will give instructions, tell you when to begin, check to see that you are marking your answer sheet correctly, and so on. He is not there to guard you, although he will see that your competitors do not take unfair advantage. He wants to help you do your best.

### 2) Listen to all instructions

Don't jump the gun! Wait until you understand all directions. In most civil service tests you get more time than you need to answer the questions. So don't be in a hurry. Read each word of instructions until you clearly understand the meaning. Study the examples, listen to all announcements and follow directions. Ask questions if you do not understand what to do.

### 3) Identify your papers

Civil service exams are usually identified by number only. You will be assigned a number; you must not put your name on your test papers. Be sure to copy your number correctly. Since more than one exam may be given, copy your exact examination title.

### 4) Plan your time

Unless you are told that a test is a "speed" or "rate of work" test, speed itself is usually not important. Time enough to answer all the questions will be provided, but this does not mean that you have all day. An overall time limit has been set. Divide the total time (in minutes) by the number of questions to determine the approximate time you have for each question.

### 5) Do not linger over difficult questions

If you come across a difficult question, mark it with a paper clip (useful to have along) and come back to it when you have been through the booklet. One caution if you do this – be sure to skip a number on your answer sheet as well. Check often to be sure that you have not lost your place and that you are marking in the row numbered the same as the question you are answering.

### 6) Read the questions

Be sure you know what the question asks! Many capable people are unsuccessful because they failed to *read* the questions correctly.

### 7) Answer all questions

Unless you have been instructed that a penalty will be deducted for incorrect answers, it is better to guess than to omit a question.

### 8) Speed tests

It is often better NOT to guess on speed tests. It has been found that on timed tests people are tempted to spend the last few seconds before time is called in marking answers at random – without even reading them – in the hope of picking up a few extra points. To discourage this practice, the instructions may warn you that your score will be "corrected" for guessing. That is, a penalty will be applied. The incorrect answers will be deducted from the correct ones, or some other penalty formula will be used.

### 9) Review your answers

If you finish before time is called, go back to the questions you guessed or omitted to give them further thought. Review other answers if you have time.

### 10) Return your test materials

If you are ready to leave before others have finished or time is called, take ALL your materials to the monitor and leave quietly. Never take any test material with you. The monitor can discover whose papers are not complete, and taking a test booklet may be grounds for disqualification.


## VIII. EXAMINATION TECHNIQUES

1) Read the general instructions carefully. These are usually printed on the first page of the exam booklet. As a rule, these instructions refer to the timing of the examination; the fact that you should not start work until the signal and must stop work at a signal, etc. If there are any *special* instructions, such as a choice of questions to be answered, make sure that you note this instruction carefully.

2) When you are ready to start work on the examination, that is as soon as the signal has been given, read the instructions to each question booklet, underline any key words or phrases, such as *least, best, outline, describe* and the like. In this way you will tend to answer as requested rather than discover on reviewing your paper that you *listed without describing*, that you selected the *worst* choice rather than the *best* choice, etc.

3) If the examination is of the objective or multiple-choice type – that is, each question will also give a series of possible answers: A, B, C or D, and you are called upon to select the best answer and write the letter next to that answer on your answer paper – it is advisable to start answering each question in turn. There may be anywhere from 50 to 100 such questions in the three or four hours allotted and you can see how much time would be taken if you read through all the questions before beginning to answer any. Furthermore, if you come across a question or group of questions which you know would be difficult to answer, it would undoubtedly affect your handling of all the other questions.

4) If the examination is of the essay type and contains but a few questions, it is a moot point as to whether you should read all the questions before starting to answer any one. Of course, if you are given a choice – say five out of seven and the like – then it is essential to read all the questions so you can eliminate the two that are most difficult. If, however, you are asked to answer all the questions, there may be danger in trying to answer the easiest one first because you may find that you will spend too much time on it. The best technique is to answer the first question, then proceed to the second, etc.

5) Time your answers. Before the exam begins, write down the time it started, then add the time allowed for the examination and write down the time it must be completed, then divide the time available somewhat as follows:
    - If 3-1/2 hours are allowed, that would be 210 minutes. If you have 80 objective-type questions, that would be an average of 2-1/2 minutes per question. Allow yourself no more than 2 minutes per question, or a total of 160 minutes, which will permit about 50 minutes to review.
    - If for the time allotment of 210 minutes there are 7 essay questions to answer, that would average about 30 minutes a question. Give yourself only 25 minutes per question so that you have about 35 minutes to review.

6) The most important instruction is to *read each question* and make sure you know what is wanted. The second most important instruction is to *time yourself properly* so that you answer every question. The third most important instruction is to *answer every question*. Guess if you have to but include something for each question. Remember that you will receive no credit for a blank and will probably receive some credit if you write something in answer to an essay question. If you guess a letter – say "B" for a multiple-choice question – you may have guessed right. If you leave a blank as an answer to a multiple-choice question, the examiners may respect your feelings but it will not add a point to your score. Some exams may penalize you for wrong answers, so in such cases *only*, you may not want to guess unless you have some basis for your answer.

7) Suggestions
    a. Objective-type questions
        1. Examine the question booklet for proper sequence of pages and questions
        2. Read all instructions carefully
        3. Skip any question which seems too difficult; return to it after all other questions have been answered
        4. Apportion your time properly; do not spend too much time on any single question or group of questions

5. Note and underline key words – *all, most, fewest, least, best, worst, same, opposite,* etc.
6. Pay particular attention to negatives
7. Note unusual option, e.g., unduly long, short, complex, different or similar in content to the body of the question
8. Observe the use of "hedging" words – *probably, may, most likely,* etc.
9. Make sure that your answer is put next to the same number as the question
10. Do not second-guess unless you have good reason to believe the second answer is definitely more correct
11. Cross out original answer if you decide another answer is more accurate; do not erase until you are ready to hand your paper in
12. Answer all questions; guess unless instructed otherwise
13. Leave time for review

b. Essay questions
1. Read each question carefully
2. Determine exactly what is wanted. Underline key words or phrases.
3. Decide on outline or paragraph answer
4. Include many different points and elements unless asked to develop any one or two points or elements
5. Show impartiality by giving pros and cons unless directed to select one side only
6. Make and write down any assumptions you find necessary to answer the questions
7. Watch your English, grammar, punctuation and choice of words
8. Time your answers; don't crowd material

8) Answering the essay question

Most essay questions can be answered by framing the specific response around several key words or ideas. Here are a few such key words or ideas:

M's: manpower, materials, methods, money, management
P's: purpose, program, policy, plan, procedure, practice, problems, pitfalls, personnel, public relations

a. Six basic steps in handling problems:
1. Preliminary plan and background development
2. Collect information, data and facts
3. Analyze and interpret information, data and facts
4. Analyze and develop solutions as well as make recommendations
5. Prepare report and sell recommendations
6. Install recommendations and follow up effectiveness

b. Pitfalls to avoid
1. *Taking things for granted* – A statement of the situation does not necessarily imply that each of the elements is necessarily true; for example, a complaint may be invalid and biased so that all that can be taken for granted is that a complaint has been registered

2. *Considering only one side of a situation* – Wherever possible, indicate several alternatives and then point out the reasons you selected the best one
3. *Failing to indicate follow up* – Whenever your answer indicates action on your part, make certain that you will take proper follow-up action to see how successful your recommendations, procedures or actions turn out to be
4. *Taking too long in answering any single question* – Remember to time your answers properly

## IX. AFTER THE TEST

Scoring procedures differ in detail among civil service jurisdictions although the general principles are the same. Whether the papers are hand-scored or graded by machine we have described, they are nearly always graded by number. That is, the person who marks the paper knows only the number – never the name – of the applicant. Not until all the papers have been graded will they be matched with names. If other tests, such as training and experience or oral interview ratings have been given, scores will be combined. Different parts of the examination usually have different weights. For example, the written test might count 60 percent of the final grade, and a rating of training and experience 40 percent. In many jurisdictions, veterans will have a certain number of points added to their grades.

After the final grade has been determined, the names are placed in grade order and an eligible list is established. There are various methods for resolving ties between those who get the same final grade – probably the most common is to place first the name of the person whose application was received first. Job offers are made from the eligible list in the order the names appear on it. You will be notified of your grade and your rank as soon as all these computations have been made. This will be done as rapidly as possible.

People who are found to meet the requirements in the announcement are called "eligibles." Their names are put on a list of eligible candidates. An eligible's chances of getting a job depend on how high he stands on this list and how fast agencies are filling jobs from the list.

When a job is to be filled from a list of eligibles, the agency asks for the names of people on the list of eligibles for that job. When the civil service commission receives this request, it sends to the agency the names of the three people highest on this list. Or, if the job to be filled has specialized requirements, the office sends the agency the names of the top three persons who meet these requirements from the general list.

The appointing officer makes a choice from among the three people whose names were sent to him. If the selected person accepts the appointment, the names of the others are put back on the list to be considered for future openings.

That is the rule in hiring from all kinds of eligible lists, whether they are for typist, carpenter, chemist, or something else. For every vacancy, the appointing officer has his choice of any one of the top three eligibles on the list. This explains why the person whose name is on top of the list sometimes does not get an appointment when some of the persons lower on the list do. If the appointing officer chooses the second or third eligible, the No. 1 eligible does not get a job at once, but stays on the list until he is appointed or the list is terminated.

## X. HOW TO PASS THE INTERVIEW TEST

The examination for which you applied requires an oral interview test. You have already taken the written test and you are now being called for the interview test – the final part of the formal examination.

You may think that it is not possible to prepare for an interview test and that there are no procedures to follow during an interview. Our purpose is to point out some things you can do in advance that will help you and some good rules to follow and pitfalls to avoid while you are being interviewed.

*What is an interview supposed to test?*

The written examination is designed to test the technical knowledge and competence of the candidate; the oral is designed to evaluate intangible qualities, not readily measured otherwise, and to establish a list showing the relative fitness of each candidate – as measured against his competitors – for the position sought. Scoring is not on the basis of "right" and "wrong," but on a sliding scale of values ranging from "not passable" to "outstanding." As a matter of fact, it is possible to achieve a relatively low score without a single "incorrect" answer because of evident weakness in the qualities being measured.

Occasionally, an examination may consist entirely of an oral test – either an individual or a group oral. In such cases, information is sought concerning the technical knowledges and abilities of the candidate, since there has been no written examination for this purpose. More commonly, however, an oral test is used to supplement a written examination.

*Who conducts interviews?*

The composition of oral boards varies among different jurisdictions. In nearly all, a representative of the personnel department serves as chairman. One of the members of the board may be a representative of the department in which the candidate would work. In some cases, "outside experts" are used, and, frequently, a businessman or some other representative of the general public is asked to serve. Labor and management or other special groups may be represented. The aim is to secure the services of experts in the appropriate field.

However the board is composed, it is a good idea (and not at all improper or unethical) to ascertain in advance of the interview who the members are and what groups they represent. When you are introduced to them, you will have some idea of their backgrounds and interests, and at least you will not stutter and stammer over their names.

*What should be done before the interview?*

While knowledge about the board members is useful and takes some of the surprise element out of the interview, there is other preparation which is more substantive. It *is* possible to prepare for an oral interview – in several ways:

**1) Keep a copy of your application and review it carefully before the interview**

This may be the only document before the oral board, and the starting point of the interview. Know what education and experience you have listed there, and the sequence and dates of all of it. Sometimes the board will ask you to review the highlights of your experience for them; you should not have to hem and haw doing it.

**2) Study the class specification and the examination announcement**

Usually, the oral board has one or both of these to guide them. The qualities, characteristics or knowledges required by the position sought are stated in these documents. They offer valuable clues as to the nature of the oral interview. For example, if the job involves supervisory responsibilities, the announcement will usually indicate that knowledge of modern supervisory methods and the qualifications of the candidate as a supervisor will be tested. If so, you can expect such questions, frequently in the form of a hypothetical situation which you are expected to solve. NEVER go into an oral without knowledge of the duties and responsibilities of the job you seek.

### 3) Think through each qualification required

Try to visualize the kind of questions you would ask if you were a board member. How well could you answer them? Try especially to appraise your own knowledge and background in each area, *measured against the job sought*, and identify any areas in which you are weak. Be critical and realistic – do not flatter yourself.

### 4) Do some general reading in areas in which you feel you may be weak

For example, if the job involves supervision and your past experience has NOT, some general reading in supervisory methods and practices, particularly in the field of human relations, might be useful. Do NOT study agency procedures or detailed manuals. The oral board will be testing your understanding and capacity, not your memory.

### 5) Get a good night's sleep and watch your general health and mental attitude

You will want a clear head at the interview. Take care of a cold or any other minor ailment, and of course, no hangovers.

*What should be done on the day of the interview?*

Now comes the day of the interview itself. Give yourself plenty of time to get there. Plan to arrive somewhat ahead of the scheduled time, particularly if your appointment is in the fore part of the day. If a previous candidate fails to appear, the board might be ready for you a bit early. By early afternoon an oral board is almost invariably behind schedule if there are many candidates, and you may have to wait. Take along a book or magazine to read, or your application to review, but leave any extraneous material in the waiting room when you go in for your interview. In any event, relax and compose yourself.

The matter of dress is important. The board is forming impressions about you – from your experience, your manners, your attitude, and your appearance. Give your personal appearance careful attention. Dress your best, but not your flashiest. Choose conservative, appropriate clothing, and be sure it is immaculate. This is a business interview, and your appearance should indicate that you regard it as such. Besides, being well groomed and properly dressed will help boost your confidence.

Sooner or later, someone will call your name and escort you into the interview room. *This is it.* From here on you are on your own. It is too late for any more preparation. But remember, you asked for this opportunity to prove your fitness, and you are here because your request was granted.

*What happens when you go in?*

The usual sequence of events will be as follows: The clerk (who is often the board stenographer) will introduce you to the chairman of the oral board, who will introduce you to the other members of the board. Acknowledge the introductions before you sit down. Do not be surprised if you find a microphone facing you or a stenotypist sitting by. Oral interviews are usually recorded in the event of an appeal or other review.

Usually the chairman of the board will open the interview by reviewing the highlights of your education and work experience from your application – primarily for the benefit of the other members of the board, as well as to get the material into the record. Do not interrupt or comment unless there is an error or significant misinterpretation; if that is the case, do not hesitate. But do not quibble about insignificant matters. Also, he will usually ask you some question about your education, experience or your present job – partly to get you to start talking and to establish the interviewing "rapport." He may start the actual questioning, or turn it over to one of the other members. Frequently, each member undertakes the questioning on a particular area, one in which he is perhaps most competent, so you can expect each member to participate in the examination. Because time is limited, you may also expect some rather abrupt switches in the direction the questioning takes, so do not be upset by it. Normally, a board member will not pursue a single line of questioning unless he discovers a particular strength or weakness.

After each member has participated, the chairman will usually ask whether any member has any further questions, then will ask you if you have anything you wish to add. Unless you are expecting this question, it may floor you. Worse, it may start you off on an extended, extemporaneous speech. The board is not usually seeking more information. The question is principally to offer you a last opportunity to present further qualifications or to indicate that you have nothing to add. So, if you feel that a significant qualification or characteristic has been overlooked, it is proper to point it out in a sentence or so. Do not compliment the board on the thoroughness of their examination – they have been sketchy, and you know it. If you wish, merely say, "No thank you, I have nothing further to add." This is a point where you can "talk yourself out" of a good impression or fail to present an important bit of information. Remember, *you close the interview yourself.*

The chairman will then say, "That is all, Mr. _____, thank you." Do not be startled; the interview is over, and quicker than you think. Thank him, gather your belongings and take your leave. Save your sigh of relief for the other side of the door.

*How to put your best foot forward*

Throughout this entire process, you may feel that the board individually and collectively is trying to pierce your defenses, seek out your hidden weaknesses and embarrass and confuse you. Actually, this is not true. They are obliged to make an appraisal of your qualifications for the job you are seeking, and they want to see you in your best light. Remember, they must interview all candidates and a non-cooperative candidate may become a failure in spite of their best efforts to bring out his qualifications. Here are 15 suggestions that will help you:

1) **Be natural – Keep your attitude confident, not cocky**

If you are not confident that you can do the job, do not expect the board to be. Do not apologize for your weaknesses, try to bring out your strong points. The board is interested in a positive, not negative, presentation. Cockiness will antagonize any board member and make him wonder if you are covering up a weakness by a false show of strength.

2) **Get comfortable, but don't lounge or sprawl**

Sit erectly but not stiffly. A careless posture may lead the board to conclude that you are careless in other things, or at least that you are not impressed by the importance of the occasion. Either conclusion is natural, even if incorrect. Do not fuss with your clothing, a pencil or an ashtray. Your hands may occasionally be useful to emphasize a point; do not let them become a point of distraction.

3) **Do not wisecrack or make small talk**

This is a serious situation, and your attitude should show that you consider it as such. Further, the time of the board is limited – they do not want to waste it, and neither should you.

### 4) Do not exaggerate your experience or abilities

In the first place, from information in the application or other interviews and sources, the board may know more about you than you think. Secondly, you probably will not get away with it. An experienced board is rather adept at spotting such a situation, so do not take the chance.

### 5) If you know a board member, do not make a point of it, yet do not hide it

Certainly you are not fooling him, and probably not the other members of the board. Do not try to take advantage of your acquaintanceship – it will probably do you little good.

### 6) Do not dominate the interview

Let the board do that. They will give you the clues – do not assume that you have to do all the talking. Realize that the board has a number of questions to ask you, and do not try to take up all the interview time by showing off your extensive knowledge of the answer to the first one.

### 7) Be attentive

You only have 20 minutes or so, and you should keep your attention at its sharpest throughout. When a member is addressing a problem or question to you, give him your undivided attention. Address your reply principally to him, but do not exclude the other board members.

### 8) Do not interrupt

A board member may be stating a problem for you to analyze. He will ask you a question when the time comes. Let him state the problem, and wait for the question.

### 9) Make sure you understand the question

Do not try to answer until you are sure what the question is. If it is not clear, restate it in your own words or ask the board member to clarify it for you. However, do not haggle about minor elements.

### 10) Reply promptly but not hastily

A common entry on oral board rating sheets is "candidate responded readily," or "candidate hesitated in replies." Respond as promptly and quickly as you can, but do not jump to a hasty, ill-considered answer.

### 11) Do not be peremptory in your answers

A brief answer is proper – but do not fire your answer back. That is a losing game from your point of view. The board member can probably ask questions much faster than you can answer them.

### 12) Do not try to create the answer you think the board member wants

He is interested in what kind of mind you have and how it works – not in playing games. Furthermore, he can usually spot this practice and will actually grade you down on it.

### 13) Do not switch sides in your reply merely to agree with a board member

Frequently, a member will take a contrary position merely to draw you out and to see if you are willing and able to defend your point of view. Do not start a debate, yet do not surrender a good position. If a position is worth taking, it is worth defending.

**14) Do not be afraid to admit an error in judgment if you are shown to be wrong**

The board knows that you are forced to reply without any opportunity for careful consideration. Your answer may be demonstrably wrong. If so, admit it and get on with the interview.

**15) Do not dwell at length on your present job**

The opening question may relate to your present assignment. Answer the question but do not go into an extended discussion. You are being examined for a *new* job, not your present one. As a matter of fact, try to phrase ALL your answers in terms of the job for which you are being examined.

*Basis of Rating*

Probably you will forget most of these "do's" and "don'ts" when you walk into the oral interview room. Even remembering them all will not ensure you a passing grade. Perhaps you did not have the qualifications in the first place. But remembering them will help you to put your best foot forward, without treading on the toes of the board members.

Rumor and popular opinion to the contrary notwithstanding, an oral board wants you to make the best appearance possible. They know you are under pressure – but they also want to see how you respond to it as a guide to what your reaction would be under the pressures of the job you seek. They will be influenced by the degree of poise you display, the personal traits you show and the manner in which you respond.


ABOUT THIS BOOK

This book contains tests divided into Examination Sections. Go through each test, answering every question in the margin. We have also attached a sample answer sheet at the back of the book that can be removed and used. At the end of each test look at the answer key and check your answers. On the ones you got wrong, look at the right answer choice and learn. Do not fill in the answers first. Do not memorize the questions and answers, but understand the answer and principles involved. On your test, the questions will likely be different from the samples. Questions are changed and new ones added. If you understand these past questions you should have success with any changes that arise. Tests may consist of several types of questions. We have additional books on each subject should more study be advisable or necessary for you. Finally, the more you study, the better prepared you will be. This book is intended to be the last thing you study before you walk into the examination room. Prior study of relevant texts is also recommended. NLC publishes some of these in our Fundamental Series. Knowledge and good sense are important factors in passing your exam. Good luck also helps. So now study this Passbook, absorb the material contained within and take that knowledge into the examination. Then do your best to pass that exam.

# EXAMINATION SECTION

# EXAMINATION SECTION
# TEST 1

DIRECTIONS: Each question or incomplete statement is followed by several suggested answers or completions. Select the one that BEST answers the question or completes the statement. *PRINT THE LETTER OF THE CORRECT ANSWER IN THE SPACE AT THE RIGHT.*

1. The PRIME reason for not replacing a blown fuse with another fuse having a higher rating is that the

    A. fuse will blow
    B. higher rating fuse will not fit properly
    C. designed purpose of the fuse would be lost
    D. circuit will have a higher power consumption

1.____

2. In the event of a failure to ground in a power substation, the purpose of the ground protection is to automatically

    A. ground the negative bus
    B. de-energize the 600 volt feeder
    C. de-energize all high tension feeders
    D. switch the 600 volts D.C. to another substation

2.____

3. Two common tests that are used to check a silicon diode are the _____ test and the _____ test.

    A. power dissipation; CFM
    B. calibration; surge current
    C. ohmmeter; peak reverse current
    D. thermal current rating; high voltage

3.____

4. With respect to proper safety precautions on electrical maintenance tools, it would be MOST correct to state that the tool insulation

    A. insures the safety of the user
    B. provides protection against abrasion only
    C. is of most value in a wet working area
    D. should be supplemented with a ground protection

4.____

5. The term *high dielectric strength* is normally associated with the characteristic of a

    A. transformer           B. type of insulation
    C. cable                 D. switch

5.____

6. A neon-glow lamp is a convenience and compact device used for

    A. precision ammeter protection
    B. precision wattmeter protection
    C. determining if a power circuit is alive
    D. testing the time delay of remote relays

6.____

7. In order to start motors that require high starting currents and relatively low operating currents, the starting relay should have a

    A. time delay feature
    B. floating line coil
    C. snap action feature
    D. compensating feature

8. As a power maintainer, you think that an FMI procedure should be changed in order to improve personnel safety. The MOST desirable way to submit your idea to management is by

    A. submitting it through the Employee Suggestion Plan
    B. attending the next foremen's safety meeting
    C. writing directly to the division superintendent
    D. discussing it at the next union meeting

9. As a newly appointed maintainer, you are assigned to work with a more experienced maintainer who pays no attention to the safety rules.
   The PROPER procedure would be for you to

    A. work with the maintainer but watch him very carefully
    B. ask your foreman if you could review this maintainer's safety record
    C. refuse to work with this maintainer and ask your foreman for another assignment
    D. tell the maintainer, before starting to work, that you would like him to adhere to the safety rules for his protection and yours

10. Electrical indicating instruments are USUALLY damped to prevent

    A. the needle from going off-scale
    B. the needle from reading down-scale
    C. excessive oscillation of the needle
    D. damage to the instruments if it is dropped

11. If a steel nut must stay tight under vibration, the MOST practical procedure would be to

    A. drill a hole in the nut
    B. use a self-locking nut
    C. weld the nut to the bolt
    D. stake the threads at the end of the bolt

12. A rule of the transit authority states that *employees are required to report defective equipment to their superiors, even when the maintenance of the particular piece of equipment is handled by another department.*
    The purpose of this rule is to

    A. encourage alertness
    B. fix responsibility
    C. prevent accidents
    D. take advantage of manufacturer's guarantees

13. A good practical test to determine whether or not a wetted-down motor is sufficiently dried out is a(n) _____ test.

    A. flash-over
    B. high-voltage breakdown
    C. armature resistance
    D. insulation resistance

14. To smooth pitted contacts of a D.C. feeder breaker, you should use

    A. a fine file
    B. coarse sandpaper
    C. emery cloth
    D. steel wool

15. A single-phase A.C. potential of 240 volts is required for test purposes. A 600 volt A.C. source and two identical transformers with 300 volt primaries and 120 volt secondaries are available.
    The transformers should be connected with primaries in _____, secondaries in _____.

    A. series; series
    B. series; parallel
    C. parallel; series
    D. parallel; parallel

16. Your foreman gives you verbal directions on how to dismantle some equipment. After a period of time, you find that you cannot proceed with the dismantling in accordance with the procedure outlined by your foreman.
    Your BEST course of action is to

    A. use your own judgment
    B. ask your foreman for a further explanation
    C. discuss it with your helper
    D. discuss it with another maintainer

17. Before work is started on any power equipment, a Hold-Off tag MUST be

    A. in the System Operator's office
    B. attached to the piece of equipment to be worked on
    C. in the personal possession of the man in charge of the work
    D. attached to the control switch of the equipment to be worked on

18. A *trip-free,* manually operated air circuit breaker is one which

    A. does not open on sustained overloads
    B. does not open on instantaneous overloads
    C. has a defective mechanism and opens too readily
    D. can be opened by overloads while the closing handle is held in the closed position

19. Transit employees are cautioned not to use water to extinguish fires caused by high voltage arcing.
    The MOST important reason for this rule is that the water

    A. may conduct the current and create a shock hazard
    B. will cause corrosion of sensitive electrical parts
    C. would cause the fuses to blow in electrical circuits
    D. coming into contact with an electrical arc releases asphyxiating fumes

20. When lifting very heavy objects, a maintainer should have assistance and

    A. lift using only his arm muscles
    B. lift using only his back muscles
    C. lean over the object to be lifted
    D. lift making full use of his leg muscles

21. If a co-worker is in contact with a high-voltage circuit, the FIRST action taken by you should be to

    A. call the doctor
    B. call the foreman
    C. cut off the power
    D. get the first aid kit

22. The MAIN purpose of the oil in an oil-filled power transformer is to

    A. quench arcing
    B. provide insulation
    C. prevent corrosion
    D. provide lubrication

23. In an A.C. circuit, the ratio of watts to voltamperes is to

    A. load factor
    B. power factor
    C. impedance
    D. efficiency

24. The MAXIMUM current that a circuit breaker can carry continuously is determined by its

    A. maximum trip setting
    B. instantaneous trip setting
    C. rated current capacity
    D. current interrupting capacity

25. An ammeter reads 6 amperes at full scale and has an internal resistance of 0.1 ohms. If this ammeter is to be used to register 60 amperes at full scale, it MUST be supplied with a shunt of _____ ohms.

    A. 0.011    B. 0.090    C. 0.900    D. 1.000

26. A transformer built so that both the primary and the secondary currents flow through the same winding is known as a(n) _____ transformer.

    A. auto-
    B. insulating
    C. variable-ratio
    D. constant-current

27. Of the following, the factor which determines the LARGEST capacity of fuse that may be used in a given circuit is the

    A. largest size of wire beyond the fuse
    B. minimum overload expected
    C. importance of maintaining the circuit alive
    D. number of fuses previously blown in the circuit

28. The secondary windings of energized current transformers are short circuited before opening the secondary circuit to

    A. clear the secondary circuit from ground
    B. maintain the continuity of the primary circuit
    C. prevent excessive current flow in the secondary winding
    D. prevent building up a high voltage in the secondary winding

29. Four resistors having respective current ratings of 2.5, 4, 4.5, and 6 amperes are connected in series.
    If the resistors are not to be overloaded, the MAXIMUM current permissible in this circuit is _____ amperes.

    A. 2.5    B. 4.25    C. 6    D. 17

30. The proper arrangement of the following wire sizes, in the order of increasing electrical resistance, is

    A. 2; 4/0; 1/0
    B. 1/0; 4/0; 2
    C. 2; 1/0; 4/0
    D. 4/0; 1/0; 2

31. Operating instructions are issued by the department

    A. for the guidance of employees
    B. for reading when the employee is not busy
    C. as a basis for evaluating employee performance
    D. to justify penalties in case of errors in operation

32. In a balanced, three-phase, three-wire, delta-connected circuit, the line voltages are equal

    A. to the phase voltages
    B. but the line currents are unequal
    C. but the phase voltages are unequal
    D. to three times the value of the sum of the phase voltages

Questions 33-39.

DIRECTIONS: Questions 33 through 39, inclusive, refer to the D.C. wiring diagram below. Unless otherwise stated, all switches are open. Neglect the effects of the ammeter and voltmeter on the circuit.

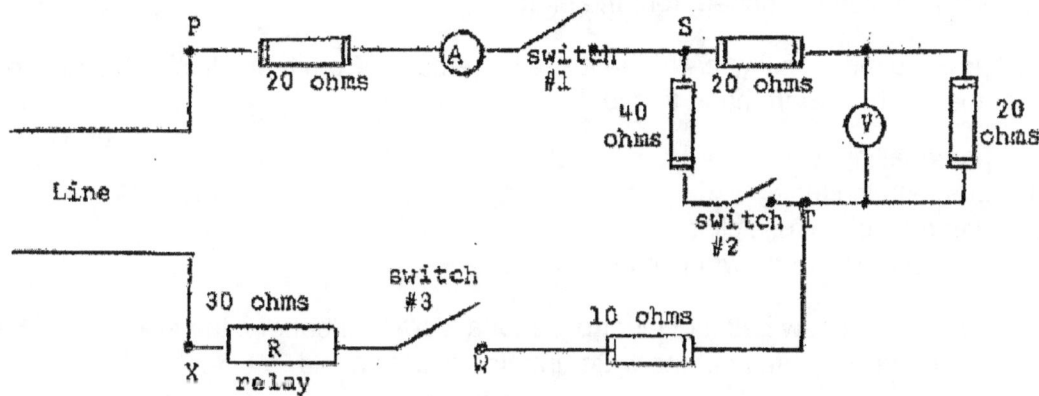

33. A circuit resistance of 100 ohms is obtained by closing switch nos.

    A. 1, 2, and 3
    B. 2 and 3
    C. 1 and 3
    D. 1 and 2

34. With all switches closed and 2 amperes flowing through the 40 ohm resistor, the line voltage is _____ volts.

    A. 80    B. 160    C. 240    D. 320

35. With all switches closed and the ammeter reading 1 ampere, the power consumed by the circuit is _____ watts.

    A. 60    B. 80    C. 100    D. 140

36. With switch nos. 1 and 3 closed and a line voltage of 100 volts D.C., the voltmeter reading should be _____ volts.

    A. 0  B. 20  C. 40  D. 80

37. The relay (R) requires at least 1.10 amperes to operate. With a line voltage of 100 volts D.C., it will be operated by closing switch nos.

    A. 1 and 2
    C. 2 and 3
    B. 1 and 3
    D. 1, 2, and 3

38. If the two lead wires to the ammeter are reversed, and all switches were closed, the

    A. ammeter should indicate zero current
    B. ammeter needle should move backwards
    C. ammeter will continue to indicate properly
    D. current in the entire circuit will be reversed

39. With all switches closed, and a line voltage of 50 V D.C., the LARGEST voltage drop should be across points

    A. P and S  B. S and T  C. T and W  D. W and X

40. Sediment found at the bottom of a lead-acid battery cell is MAINLY due to

    A. the addition of water
    B. disintegration of the container
    C. precipitation from the electrolyte
    D. active material dropped from the plates

41. Good practice requires that cartridge fuses be removed from their clips with a fuse puller rather than with the bare hand to avoid

    A. personal injury
    B. breaking the fuse
    C. damage to the fuse clips
    D. the possibility of drawing an arc

42. When preparing a new batch of electrolyte for a lead-acid battery, the acid should be poured into the water and not the water into the acid to avoid

    A. dangerous splattering
    B. corrosion of the mixing vessel
    C. making the mixture too weak
    D. making the mixture too strong

43. Feed back from a control battery to the charging generator is USUALLY guarded against by

    A. fuses in the battery charging circuit
    B. no-load protection on the charging set motor
    C. a low voltage trip on the generator circuit breaker
    D. a reverse current trip on the generator circuit breaker

44. When the control battery is *floated* on the bus of a motor-generator set, the generator is adjusted to

    A. share the constant control load equally, with the battery
    B. maintain constant line voltage regardless of the control demand
    C. stop when the battery is fully charged and start again when the battery voltage drops
    D. carry the constant load and also send a small current into the battery to keep it fully charged

45. The color of the prescribed Power Department NOT CLEAR tag is

    A. blue   B. green   C. red   D. yellow

46. On a certain voltmeter, the same scale is used for three ranges; these are 0-750, 0-300, and 0-15 volts.
    If the scale is marked only for the 0-750 volt range, a scale reading of 150 when the 300-volt range is being used corresponds to an actual voltage of _____ volts.

    A. 15   B. 60   C. 150   D. 350

47. As soon as a test potential has been removed from a piece of high voltage equipment,

    A. all safety grounds can be removed
    B. the person in charge should survey the area and remove the high voltage caution sign
    C. the equipment should be discharged to ground before anyone is allowed to come in contact with it
    D. the person in charge shall immediately inform the employee in charge of the apparatus that the test is over

48. The SMALLEST number of single-phase A.C. wattmeters required to measure the power in a three-phase, 4-wire, unbalanced delta-wye connected A.C. circuit is

    A. 4   B. 3   C. 2   D. 1

49. Before repairing an electric power tool, the preferred safety practice is to

    A. remove the power to the tool
    B. ground both sides of the power supply
    C. stand on an insulated mat
    D. place the tool on an insulated mat

50. In electrical work, the symbol Hz indicates

    A. watts per hour              B. cycles per second
    C. very high voltage           D. horsepower rating

51. The BEST immediate first aid if electrolyte splashes into the eyes when filling a storage battery is to

    A. bandage the eyes to keep out light
    B. wipe the eyes dry with a soft towel
    C. bathe the eyes with plenty of clean water
    D. induce tears to flow by staring at a bright light

52. The electrical power for each section of the subway signal system is arranged to come from either one of two supply feeders.
The MOST likely reason for this arrangement is to

    A. avoid the use of very large cables
    B. divide the load between two power plants
    C. keep the supply voltage as low as possible
    D. provide continuing service if one feeder goes dead

53. Assume a fellow employee has lost his pass and asks you to lend him your pass to be used to perform an errand for the foreman.
You should

    A. lend the pass if the foreman approves
    B. refuse because you might need the pass yourself
    C. refuse because the pass is issued for your own use only
    D. lend the pass because it is going to be used on a legitimate errand

54. In the power department, the voltage level used to differentiate between low voltage and high voltage apparatus is MOST NEARLY _____ volts.

    A. 440        B. 600        C. 750        D. 1000

55. Tools which are damaged should

    A. be used only for unimportant work
    B. be used until replacements can be obtained
    C. not be used because personal injury might result
    D. not be used because you may be held responsible for the damage

56. The BEST time to adjust the brushes on a D.C. motor is when the motor is

    A. de-energized
    B. running at no load
    C. running at full load
    D. operated as a generator with a test bank of lamps

57. You will probably be MOST highly regarded by your superiors if you show that you

    A. like your work by asking all the questions you can about it
    B. are interested in improving the job by continually offering suggestions
    C. are willing to do your share by completing assigned tasks properly and on time
    D. are on the job by volunteering information whenever you think someone has violated a safety rule

58. In standard report forms, it is advisable to print rather than write in the entries because printing generally

    A. looks better              B. is more legible
    C. occupies less space       D. is easier to do

59. The sum of 1 9/16", 3 1/2", 7 3/8", 10 3/4", and 12 5/8" is

    A. 33 11/16"                 B. 34 13/16"
    C. 35 11/16"                 D. 35 13/16"

60. A rule of the transit authority states that *Employees must be thoroughly acquainted with, and qualified to operate, all equipment which they may be required to handle in the performance of their duties.*
The probable reason for this rule is that

    A. an employee should be able to perform his duties properly
    B. all employees must be able to operate all transit equipment
    C. an employee can be kept busy operating equipment during a slow period
    D. an employee should be able to substitute for a higher titled employee at any time

---

# KEY (CORRECT ANSWERS)

| | | | |
|---|---|---|---|
| 1. C | 16. B | 31. A | 46. B |
| 2. B | 17. D | 32. A | 47. C |
| 3. C | 18. D | 33. C | 48. B |
| 4. D | 19. A | 34. D | 49. A |
| 5. B | 20. D | 35. B | 50. B |
| 6. C | 21. C | 36. B | 51. C |
| 7. A | 22. B | 37. D | 52. D |
| 8. A | 23. B | 38. B | 53. C |
| 9. D | 24. C | 39. D | 54. C |
| 10. C | 25. A | 40. D | 55. C |
| 11. B | 26. A | 41. A | 56. A |
| 12. C | 27. B | 42. A | 57. C |
| 13. D | 28. D | 43. D | 58. B |
| 14. A | 29. A | 44. D | 59. D |
| 15. A | 30. D | 45. D | 60. A |

# TEST 2

DIRECTIONS: Each question or incomplete statement is followed by several suggested answers or completions. Select the one that BEST answers the question or completes the statement. *PRINT THE LETTER OF THE CORRECT ANSWER IN THE SPACE AT THE RIGHT.*

1. The section of a mercury arc rectifier which maintains low pressure in the vacuum tank is the _____ system.

    A. pumping   B. ignition   C. excitation   D. cooling

2. The local emergency control key and lamp group located in the control room consists of a green lamp, a red lamp, a control key, a(n)

    A. select key, and an operate key
    B. white lamp, and a select key
    C. amber lamp, and a white lamp
    D. indication key, and an operate key

3. During a bakeout, of a mercury arc rectifier, a voltmeter is connected between the tank and cathode to detect arcing.
   The PROPER voltmeter to use should have a range of 0 - _____ volts _____.

    A. 30; D.C.   B. 60; D.C.   C. 150; A.C.   D. 300; A.C.

4. The purpose of the glob tube in a telemetering circuit is to provide protection should the _____ become _____.

    A. line wires; open-circuited
    B. line wires; short-circuited
    C. disc film cut-out; inoperative
    D. filament transformer; short-circuited

5. While a certain zone is being operated from the local emergency control panel in the control room, a rectifier trips off the line automatically.
   The indication obtained in the control room is a change in indicating lights from red to green and

    A. a bell signal
    B. a white light
    C. no other indication
    D. a bell signal and a white light

6. Low tension A.C. power is furnished to the substations for auxiliary equipment at

    A. 110 volts, single-phase
    B. 600 volts, single-phase
    C. 220 volts, 2-phase, 4-wire
    D. 208/120 volts, 3-phase, 4-wire

7. A common feature of devices 23R, 26H, 26L, and 26R is that ALL are actuated by

    A. current   B. pressure   C. temperature   D. voltage

8. When drawing a sample of insulating oil for test from an oil circuit breaker having a sampling cock, about two quarts of oil should be drained out before taking a sample. This is done   8.____

   A. to agitate the oil in the tank before sampling
   B. because the first two quarts always have water present
   C. to obtain sufficient oil to rinse out the sample bottle
   D. so that the sample represents the oil in the tank and not that in the drain pipe

9. A mercury arc rectifier is usually equipped with both a mercury vacuum pump and a rotary vacuum pump.   9.____
   The reason for having two pumps is that the

   A. mercury pump is not suited for continuous operation
   B. rotary pump alone cannot produce the required degree of vacuum
   C. rotary pump serves as a reserve unit in case of failure of the mercury pump
   D. mercury pump serves as a reserve unit in case of failure of the rotary pump

10. The newly installed silicon rectifiers in the NYCTA are 12-phase rather than single-phase or 3-phase rectifiers.   10.____
    One of the PRINCIPAL reasons for this is that

    A. less routine maintenance is required
    B. the cathode carries a smaller current
    C. a smoother, more even D.C. voltage is obtained
    D. an even number of phases is essential for good operation

11. Each device used in the automatic switching equipment in the power department has been assigned a *device number*. The PRIMARY purpose of the particular numbering system used is   11.____

    A. for convenience when referring to blueprints
    B. to simplify the ordering of replacement parts
    C. to indicate the function of the particular device
    D. to identify the location of the device in the substation

12. The position of all supervised units may be checked at the System Operation board at any time by pushing the _____ key.   12.____

    A. control      B. operate      C. select      D. start

13. A bake-out is GENERALLY considered necessary for a rectifier if   13.____

    A. it has been subjected to a heavy overload
    B. it has been open to the atmosphere for a long period
    C. it has been operating at light load for a long period
    D. more than three months have elapsed since a previous bake-out

14. The relief diaphragm is installed on a rectifier power transformer to provide protection agains   14.____

    A. excessive voltage              B. excessive oil pressure
    C. high vacuum                    D. high water pressure

15. When a rectifier is *held off* and disconnected from the station positive bus, the power connections to the inter-phase transformer should

    A. be connected to ground
    B. never be grounded
    C. all be tied to the negative bus
    D. be tied to the positive side of a low potential safety relay

16. In a rectifier cooling system, a section of rubber hose is used on each side of the

    A. water pump, for flexibility
    B. heat exchanger, for heat insulation
    C. surge tank, for ease of connection
    D. rectifier tank, for electrical insulation

17. The purpose of device 49A on the battery charging MG set is to

    A. adjust voltage
    B. protect the motor against overload
    C. connect the motor to the supply lines
    D. connect the generator to the control bus

18. The neutral of the interphase transformer is connected to the

    A. D.C. negative bus
    B. substation ground
    C. power transformer neutral
    D. D.C. positive bus

19. A rectifier is given a seepage test in order to determine

    A. the tightness of tank and pipe line
    B. if its cooling coils are tight
    C. the condition and amount of mercury in the chamber
    D. if the heating coils are functioning properly

20. The identifying number F14 on a cable would indicate the

    A. negative cable to zone 14
    B. supervisory cable to zone 14
    C. control cable to substation number 14
    D. battery cable to substation number 14

## KEY (CORRECT ANSWERS)

1. A
2. D
3. B
4. A
5. C

6. D
7. C
8. D
9. B
10. C

11. C
12. D
13. B
14. B
15. B

16. D
17. B
18. A
19. A
20. B

# TEST 3

DIRECTIONS: Each question or incomplete statement is followed by several suggested answers or completions. Select the one that BEST answers the question or completes the statement. *PRINT THE LETTER OF THE CORRECT ANSWER IN THE SPACE AT THE RIGHT.*

1. An overspeed device on a rotary converter having synchronous speed of 280 rpm is set to operate at 15% overspeed. It will operate when the speed of the rotary reaches about _____ rpm.  1.____

   A.  240  B.  295  C.  320  D.  360

2. On receiving an emergency alarm at a substation, after noting the code signal and the time, the NEXT thing the substation operator should do is  2.____

   A. notify system operation office
   B. restore the *drop* switch to its *up* position
   C. check that all breakers have opened that should have opened

3. One purpose of the milliammeter on the emergency alarm panel in a substation is to  3.____

   A. indicate when all tracks are de-energized
   B. provide a check on the gong code signal
   C. measure the tripping current for the feeder breakers
   D. give an indication that the subway circuit is closed

4. When cleaning a rotary converter, it is MOST correct to  4.____

   A. carefully wipe the A.C. and D.C. brushes with a rag
   B. carefully blow down the A.C. and D.C. brushes with compressed air
   C. lift the brushes from the brush boxes and wipe the contact surfaces
   D. carefully clean the A.C. and D.C. brush holders with a vacuum cleaner

5. When shutting down a rotary converter, it is common practice to adjust the power factor to unity  5.____

   A. *before* opening the oil circuit breaker
   B. *before* opening the positive switch
   C. *after* opening the equalizer breaker or switch
   D. *after* opening the battery switch on the rotary converter panel

6. A rotary converter is used to  6.____

   A. change A.C. power into D.C. power
   B. step-down the substation against abnormal conditions
   C. protect the substation against abnormal conditions
   D. equalize the A.C. power input with the D.C. power output

7. The pilot cell of a substation control battery is that cell which  7.____

   A. is the middle cell for all batteries
   B. gives the lowest voltage reading on test
   C. gives the highest specific gravity reading on test
   D. is selected as the representative cell for the whole battery

14

8. The difference between the JR36 breaker, when used as device 72 rather than device 54, is that as device 72 the breaker

   A. is trip-free
   B. has a lower voltage rating
   C. has a lower amperage rating
   D. has inductive shunts and a bucking bar

9. When a rotary converter is started as a D.C. motor, it is brought up to speed

   A. with its shunt field separate excited
   B. shunt field of self-excited
   C. with the use of a field reversing switch
   D. without the use of any starting resistance

10. A device used in some substations to convert A.C. to D.C. for starting purposes is called a(n)

    A. equalizer
    B. motor-generator set
    C. field transfer switch
    D. rotary power transformer

11. When starting a rotary converter by means of an induction motor, the induction motor

    A. is adjusted so that its synchronous speed is less than the rotary speed
    B. is mounted on the shaft of the rotary and has two less poles than the rotary
    C. has its speed controlled for synchronization by adjusting the A.C. voltage to the motor
    D. affects the rotary power factor by a change in the induction motor's shunt field excitation

12. The PRINCIPAL use of the main blowers in a substation is to

    A. cool the transformers
    B. ventilate the station
    C. cool the rotary converters
    D. provide compressed air to blow out the rotaries

13. The particular rotary to be used under light-load conditions is usually varied from time to time in a multi-unit station.
    The BEST reason for doing this is so that

    A. the power factor can be kept uniform
    B. all the rotaries receive about the same wear
    C. the operator can become experienced on all the rotaries
    D. the rotary performances can be compared with one another

14. The nominal speed of a rotary converter is governed by the

    A. A.C. voltage and D.C. load
    B. D.C. load and the shunt field current
    C. excitation of the shunt field and the A.C. voltage
    D. frequency of the A.C. supply and the number of poles

15. A rotary, started as a D.C. motor, is brought into synchronism by adjusting the

    A. D.C. bus voltage
    B. rotary power factor
    C. shunt field current
    D. A.C. supply frequency

16. When a rotary converter is started from the A.C. side, all the D.C. brushes are usually raised from the commutator except for one positive and one negative brush. These two brushes are left in contact with the commutator to

    A. permit speed control
    B. provide relay protection
    C. indicate the D.C. polarity
    D. maintain unity power factor

17. When a rotary converter is being synchronized, the oil circuit breaker control switch should be closed at the instant the synchroscope pointer

    A. points horizontally to the left
    B. points horizontally to the right
    C. reaches the vertically upward position
    D. reaches the vertically downward position

18. When shutting down a rotary converter during light load hours, the FIRST thing you should do after reducing the load is to

    A. trip the positive breaker
    B. open the oil circuit breaker
    C. open the battery switch
    D. close the transformer dampers

19. When dielectric tests indicate the presence of water in transformer oil, the water is USUALLY removed by having the oil

    A. boiled
    B. distilled
    C. filtered
    D. chemically treated

20. Rotary converters are NEVER started

    A. as synchronous motors
    B. from the D.C. bus as shunt motors
    C. by a direct connected induction motor
    D. as series motors from the D.C. bus

## KEY (CORRECT ANSWERS)

1. C
2. C
3. D
4. B
5. A

6. A
7. D
8. D
9. A
10. B

11. B
12. A
13. B
14. D
15. C

16. C
17. C
18. A
19. C
20. D

# EXAMINATION SECTION
# TEST 1

DIRECTIONS: Each question or incomplete statement is followed by several suggested answers or completions. Select the one that BEST answers the question or completes the statement. *PRINT THE LETTER OF THE CORRECT ANSWER IN THE SPACE AT THE RIGHT.*

1. If a partial short circuit develops in the operating coil of an a.c. magnetic contactor in service,  1._____

    A. the current through the coil will be reduced
    B. the contacts will spark excessively
    C. the coil will tend to become overheated
    D. no current will flow through the coil

2. The abbreviation P.I.L.C. is used to describe a type of  2._____

    A. contact rail           B. cable
    C. conduit                D. breaker

3. In general, the MAIN concern in the operation of transformers is the transformer  3._____

    A. primary voltage        B. exciting current
    C. core loss              D. temperature

4. A millivoltmeter with a shunt is used in a d.c. circuit to measure  4._____

    A. current                B. voltage
    C. resistance             D. power

5. Maintenance instructions issued by the Power Department are for  5._____

    A. justifying penalties in case of errors in maintenance
    B. the evaluation of employee performance
    C. the guidance of the employees
    D. the use of new employees only

6. The term *ambient temperature* means the  6._____

    A. minimum temperature rise of an electrical unit
    B. maximum temperature rise of an electrical unit
    C. outdoor air temperature
    D. air temperature about an electrical unit

7. For a given 3-phase transformer, the connection giving the HIGHEST secondary voltage is _____ primary, _____ secondary.  7._____

    A. delta; wye             B. delta; delta
    C. wye; wye               D. wye; delta

8. An induction motor designed to operate on a 60-cycle system at a speed of 900 rpm would have _____ poles.  8._____

    A. 2        B. 4        C. 6        D. 8

19

9. Decreasing the gap between the armature and pole faces of an a.c. magnetic contactor will _____ voltage.

   A. lower the drop out
   B. lower the pick up
   C. raise the drop out
   D. raise the pick up

10. The rated current capacity of a circuit breaker is the

    A. maximum current the breaker can carry continuously
    B. minimum current at which the breaker can be set to trip
    C. maximum current it can carry without tripping
    D. maximum current it can interrupt successfully

11. The MAIN purpose of the green and red indicating lamps on a high tension feeder control panel is to indicate whether the

    A. control circuit is open or closed
    B. trip coil is energized or de-energized
    C. circuit breaker is open or closed
    D. closing coil is energized or de-energized

12. A blown fuse in one supply lead to a three-phase induction motor would cause

    A. the motor to stop
    B. a reversal of rotation
    C. an increase in speed
    D. overheating of the stator windings

13. In an accident report, the information which may be MOST useful in decreasing the recurrence of similar type accidents is the

    A. extent of injuries sustained
    B. time the accident happened
    C. number of people involved
    D. cause of the accident

14. The purpose of the lead sheath on an underground power cable is to

    A. make the cable more flexible
    B. provide protection for the insulation
    C. allow for expansion of the insulating compound
    D. prevent the cable from being bent too sharply

15. Good practice requires that cartridge fuses be removed from their clips with a fuse puller rather than with the bare hand to avoid

    A. damage to the fuse clips
    B. personal injury
    C. breakage of the fuse
    D. possibility of drawing an arc

16. The secondary windings of energized current transformers are shorted before opening the secondary circuit to    16._____

    A. maintain the continuity of the primary circuit
    B. prevent excessive current flow in the secondary winding
    C. prevent the secondary voltage from reaching an abnormally high value
    D. prevent false operation of the protective devices

17. A certain relay coil is suspected of having some turns short circuited. To determine if this is true, you should    17._____

    A. check the winding for continuity by means of a test lamp
    B. measure the resistance and compare with the specified resistance
    C. measure the insulation resistance
    D. check the coil for grounds

18. The voltage in a high tension a.c. circuit is USUALLY measured by means of a voltmeter and a    18._____

    A. multiplier
    B. shunt
    C. bridge
    D. potential transformer

19. A high tension feeder is always phased out before connecting to the bus    19._____

    A. if it has been cut and repaired
    B. each time it has been out of service
    C. after the substation has gone out a.c.
    D. when the relay setting has been changed

20. Electrical indicating instruments are USUALLY damped to prevent    20._____

    A. excessive oscillation of the pointer
    B. the instrument from drying out
    C. the pointer from going off scale
    D. damage to the instrument if dropped

21. Feedback from a control battery to the charging generator is USUALLY guarded against by    21._____

    A. a low voltage trip on the generator circuit breaker
    B. no-load protection on the charging set motor
    C. a reverse current trip on the generator circuit breaker
    D. fuses in the battery charging circuit

22. When preparing a new batch of electrolyte for a lead-acid battery, the sulphuric acid should be poured into the water and not the water into the acid to avoid    22._____

    A. making the mixture too strong
    B. corrosion of the mixing vessel
    C. dangerous splattering
    D. making the mixture too weak

Questions 23-29.

DIRECTIONS: Questions 23 through 29, inclusive, refer to the following diagram. Note that the line current is 6 amperes as shown.

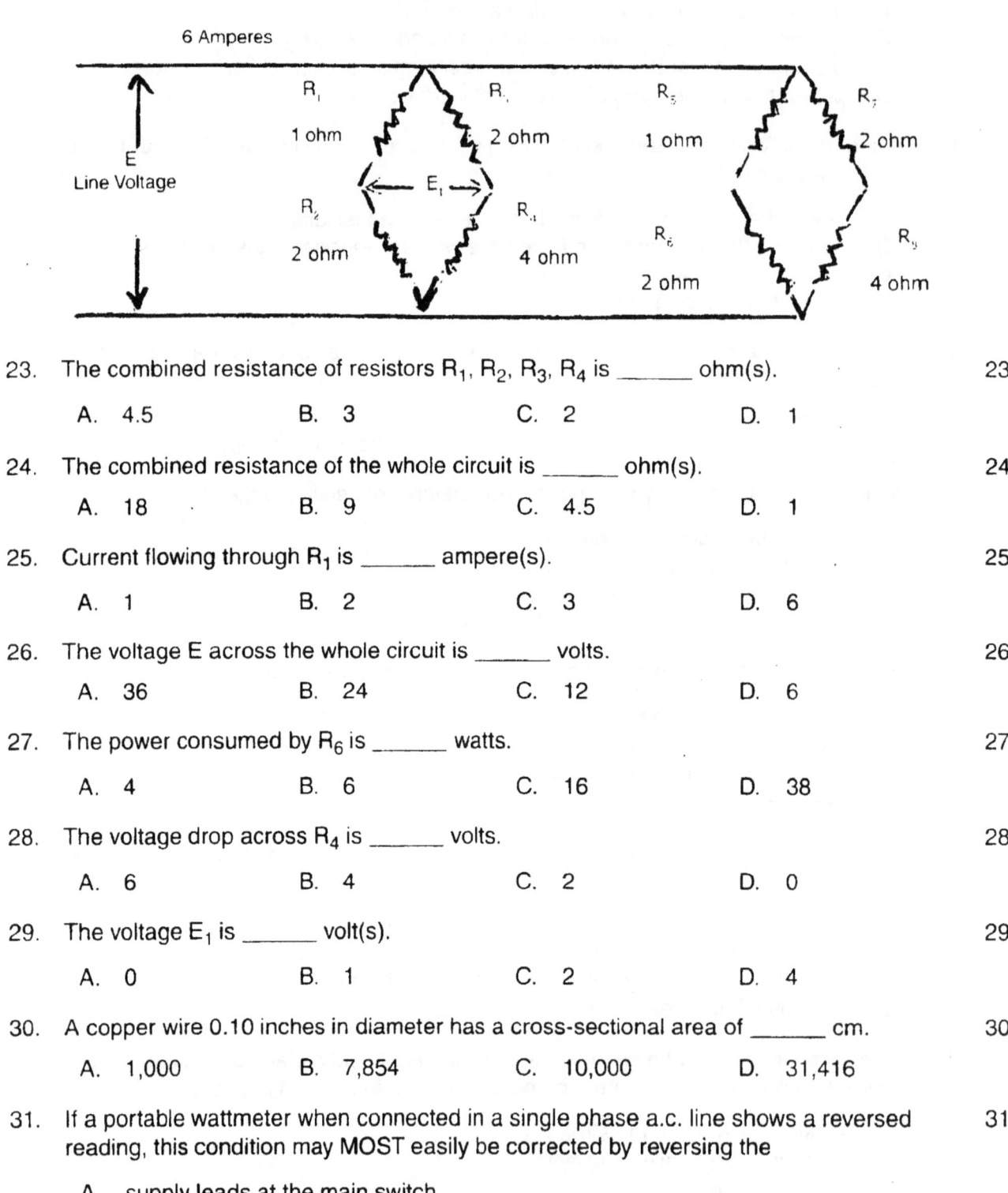

23. The combined resistance of resistors $R_1$, $R_2$, $R_3$, $R_4$ is _____ ohm(s).

    A. 4.5    B. 3    C. 2    D. 1

24. The combined resistance of the whole circuit is _____ ohm(s).

    A. 18    B. 9    C. 4.5    D. 1

25. Current flowing through $R_1$ is _____ ampere(s).

    A. 1    B. 2    C. 3    D. 6

26. The voltage E across the whole circuit is _____ volts.

    A. 36    B. 24    C. 12    D. 6

27. The power consumed by $R_6$ is _____ watts.

    A. 4    B. 6    C. 16    D. 38

28. The voltage drop across $R_4$ is _____ volts.

    A. 6    B. 4    C. 2    D. 0

29. The voltage $E_1$ is _____ volt(s).

    A. 0    B. 1    C. 2    D. 4

30. A copper wire 0.10 inches in diameter has a cross-sectional area of _____ cm.

    A. 1,000    B. 7,854    C. 10,000    D. 31,416

31. If a portable wattmeter when connected in a single phase a.c. line shows a reversed reading, this condition may MOST easily be corrected by reversing the

    A. supply leads at the main switch
    B. current connections to the meter
    C. supply leads at the load
    D. potential connections to the meter

32. The presence of water in the oil of an oil-filled power transformer is objectionable because it will cause

    A. rusting of the electrical connections
    B. a decrease of the dielectric strength of the oil
    C. the transformer to overheat
    D. erratic operation of temperature measuring devices

33. Testing for a blown cartridge fuse by connecting a lamp across the suspected fuse will in all cases indicate a

    A. blown fuse if the lamp remains dark
    B. good fuse if the lamp remains dark
    C. blown fuse if the lamp lights
    D. good fuse if the lamp lights

34. The pick-up value of an induction type a.c. overcurrent relay is changed by means of the

    A. index lever
    B. taps in the terminal block
    C. damping magnets
    D. stationary contact

35. Laminated iron is used in transformers to

    A. increase heat radiation
    B. make assembly easier
    C. reduce eddy currents
    D. reduce permeability

36. In an a.c. circuit, the ratio of kilowatts to kilovolt-amperes is the _____ factor.

    A. power
    B. load
    C. diversity
    D. conversion

37. Overtravel of an electrically operated piece of equipment is prevented by a _____ switch.

    A. break-up
    B. limit
    C. reversing
    D. throw-over

38. If two contactors are so connected that serious trouble would result if they were both closed at the same time, they are USUALLY provided with

    A. interlocks
    B. a quick break feature
    C. protective resistors
    D. time delay elements

39. A 2,400 volt three-phase system with a grounded neutral has a phase to ground voltage of APPROXIMATELY _____ volts.

    A. 4,160    B. 1,700    C. 1,390    D. 800

40. Sediment found at the bottom of a lead-acid battery cell is MAINLY due to

    A. precipitation from the electrolyte
    B. the addition of water
    C. disintegration of the container
    D. active material dropped from the plates

## KEY (CORRECT ANSWERS)

| | | | |
|---|---|---|---|
| 1. C | 11. C | 21. C | 31. D |
| 2. B | 12. D | 22. C | 32. B |
| 3. D | 13. D | 23. C | 33. C |
| 4. A | 14. B | 24. D | 34. B |
| 5. C | 15. B | 25. B | 35. C |
| 6. D | 16. C | 26. D | 36. A |
| 7. A | 17. B | 27. A | 37. B |
| 8. D | 18. D | 28. B | 38. A |
| 9. B | 19. A | 29. A | 39. C |
| 10. A | 20. A | 30. C | 40. D |

# TEST 2

DIRECTIONS: Each question or incomplete statement is followed by several suggested answers or completions. Select the one that BEST answers the question or completes the statement. *PRINT THE LETTER OF THE CORRECT ANSWER IN THE SPACE AT THE RIGHT.*

1. In the bulb-type battery chargers, two rectifier bulbs are connected in series. The reason for this is that

    A. a single bulb has insufficient voltage output
    B. failure of one bulb allows the rectifier to operate at half load
    C. the normal charging current is too high for one bulb
    D. the two bulbs provide full wave rectification

    1.____

2. Sodium chromate is added to the rectifier cooling water specifically to

    A. prevent corrosion of the cooling circuit
    B. permit reuse of the water
    C. increase thermal conductivity
    D. decrease electrical conductivity

    2.____

3. For complete supervisory control from the system operation office, the indicating lamp group provided for each supervised unit requires _____ lamp(s).

    A. a red lamp and a green
    B. red, green, and white
    C. red, green, and amber
    D. red, green, white and amber

    3.____

4. Anode heaters are provided to keep the anode tips warmer than the temperature of the mercury vapor in a rectifier to

    A. increase the electrical conductivity of the anodes
    B. maintain the arc at light loads
    C. prevent the possible formation of cathode spots on the anodes
    D. maintain a better vacuum in the vicinity of the anodes

    4.____

5. The neutral of the interphase transformer is connected to the substation _____ bus.

    A. control    B. ground    C. negative    D. positive

    5.____

6. Multi-stage mercury vacuum pumps instead of single stage pumps are used because

    A. no rotary vacuum pump is needed
    B. they can pump successfully against a higher back pressure
    C. they require less power
    D. all stages can be of the jet type

    6.____

7. On rectifiers with motor-generators for grid excitation, the motor is supplied from the

    A. 600 volt d.c. bus          B. excitation transformer
    C. 127 volt battery           D. 208 volt auxiliary bus

    7.____

25

8. A Westinghouse rectifier will shut down and lock out if the

   A. heater thermal relay (Device 23) operates
   B. control battery voltage falls below 100 volts
   C. rise in tank pressure operates Device 63V
   D. a.c. voltage drops below a safe operating value

9. In a G.E. multi-anode rectifier, in the absence of main load, the cathode spot is maintained by excitation anodes which are energized from

   A. the auxiliary bus through a transformer
   B. a motor-generator set
   C. the current transformer in the rectifier supply lines
   D. the interphase transformer

10. On an emergency alarm, if the gong sounds only once, the PROBABLE cause is

    A. that alarm box having code signal 0-0-1 was pulled in the subway
    B. an accidental opening of the subway closed circuit
    C. an accidental opening of the recorder circuit
    D. an operation of the testing alarm box

11. In the event of a 600-volt ground in a single unit substation, Device 186 in the ground protection circuit closes its contact #4 before opening contacts #2 and #3 in order to

    A. energize the white disagreement light in system operation before breakers are tripped
    B. lock itself in the operated position
    C. insert a discharge resistance across the feeder breaker 600 volt control circuit
    D. make sure that Device #164 potential coil is energized at all times

12. The interphase transformer used with a multi-anode rectifier

    A. acts as an insulating transformer between power transformer and anodes
    B. causes the anodes to overlap in firing
    C. permits only one anode to fire at a time
    D. causes each anode to fire over a shorter period of time

13. In a single unit substation, the ground protection test switch when placed in the *test* position

    A. prevents the operation of Device #186
    B. short circuits three contacts of Device #186
    C. prevents the operation of Device #164X
    D. operates Device #164 to test the ground protection system

14. A COMMONLY used method of controlling the d.c. voltage of a rectifier is by

    A. adjusting the interphase transformer ratio
    B. varying the tank pressure
    C. inserting a rheostat in the main positive lead
    D. controlling the potential of the anode grids

15. If the supply of cooling water to a mercury vapor pump should fail, Device 23V would function to

    A. open the auxiliary water valve
    B. start the reserve mercury pump
    C. open the pump heater circuit
    D. close the 63V operating circuit

16. In the emergency alarm circuit, the coil of the 180 relay is connected in series with the

    A. emergency alarm boxes in the subway
    B. coils of the 180X relays
    C. recorder relays
    D. 301 relays controlling the d.c. feeder breakers

17. A mercury arc rectifier is NOT provided with protection against

    A. a.c. undervoltage
    B. d.c. reverse current
    C. going on the line with reversed polarity
    D. operating at a temperature below a predetermined minimum

18. The cooling water for a mercury pump is NOT obtained from the rectifier recirculating system because the

    A. pump would heat the water up excessively
    B. pump operates most effectively at a lower temperature than the rectifier
    C. pump would use too much of the recirculating water
    D. water might become contaminated by the mercury

19. In the supervisory control synchronizing circuit, the selectors are made to stop at the selected unit by operating the select key (SK) to _____ to the corresponding selector point.

    A. apply positive potential
    B. apply negative potential
    C. apply ground potential
    D. open the circuit

20. When the telemetering equipment is NOT connected to the line, but is in service, the

    A. rectifier filament transformer is de-energized
    B. telemetering current transformer is short-circuited
    C. transmitter is connected to the current transformer at all times
    D. glow tube is short-circuited

21. A time delay in the operation of Device 164X on the ground protection circuit is obtained by

    A. an air dash-pot
    B. spring damping of the moving element
    C. an aluminum disc rotating between the poles of permanent magnets
    D. a 36 watt lamp in parallel with the coil

22. One of the functions of the surge tank in a rectifier recirculating cooling system is to

    A. aerate the recirculating water
    B. cool the recirculating water
    C. allow for expansion of the recirculating water
    D. provide the pressure to circulate the water

23. Two general types of telemetering circuits are used in the TS. The CHIEF difference between the two circuits is in the

    A. type of rectifier used
    B. type of protection provided against overvoltage
    C. calibration of the milliammeter
    D. supervisory selector equipment

24. If the closed series circuit in the subway should remain open after a false emergency alarm, the d.c. feeder breakers CANNOT be restored by supervisory control until the

    A. subway circuit is short-circuited by the operation of Device 162 (timer)
    B. reset switch (push-button) for Device 162 has been operated
    C. closed series circuit has been restored and re-energized
    D. 180 relay has been reset manually

25. The undervoltage relays (Device 27) are connected

    A. between the control battery positive and negative buses
    B. between the d.c. positive bus and the negative bus
    C. to potential transformers on the low voltage side of the power transformer
    D. to potential transformers on the high voltage side of the power transformer

26. The steel vacuum chamber of a multi-anode rectifier is NOT electrically insulated from

    A. the excitation anodes      B. the main anodes
    C. the arc                    D. ground

27. The 301 relays in the control room are actuated from the system operation room through selectors joined by the supervisory _____ line.

    A. control        B. indication
    C. neutral        D. synchronizing

28. One advantage of the recirculating system over the direct system of cooling rectifiers is that

    A. fewer arc backs will occur
    B. less raw water is consumed
    C. the rectifier can be operated at a much higher temperature
    D. it is easier to detect leaks in the cooling system

29. In operating mercury arc rectifiers, the tank temperature is maintained between certain limits. If the tank temperature is too low, the

    A. pressure in the tank becomes excessive
    B. mercury vapor will be carried out to atmosphere by the vacuum pumps
    C. moisture will condense on the inner surface of the tank
    D. arc becomes unstable and may be extinguished

30. The device NOT equipped with an operation counter is #

    A. 4  B. 51  C. 52  D. 72

31. On a Westinghouse type HS 10,000 ampere circuit breaker (Device #72), discrimination between short-circuits and steady overloads is provided by means of a(n)

    A. bucking bar
    B. holding magnet
    C. laminated contact brush
    D. inductive shunt

32. When taking a mercury vacuum pump out of service for cleaning and inspection, the pump should not be opened to atmosphere until it has been allowed to cool for at least 20 to 30 minutes. This is necessary

    A. because the pump would be too hot to work on
    B. so that cooling coil unions may become easier to disconnect
    C. to allow mercury vapors to condense
    D. to prevent air from corroding the pump

33. If the a.c. motor of a battery charging motor-generator set should shut down due to overheating, the set will

    A. remain shut down until Device 49A is reset by hand
    B. restart automatically when temperature is normal
    C. restart automatically when battery voltage drops below 105 volts
    D. remain shut down while Device 42A is operated

34. The secondary disconnects on a JR-25 circuit breaker are for the purpose of connecting the breaker to

    A. the d.c. bus
    B. the d.c. outgoing feeder
    C. its control power
    D. ground

35. The condition that is LEAST likely to cause an arc back in a multi-anode mercury arc rectifier is

    A. a cathode spot on an anode
    B. high tank pressure
    C. continuous operation at low loads
    D. sustained overload

36. When drawing a sample of insulating oil for test from an oil circuit breaker having a sampling cock, about two quarts of oil should be drained out before taking a sample. This is done

    A. so that sample represents oil in the tank and not that in the drain pipe
    B. to agitate the oil in the tank before sampling
    C. to obtain sufficient oil to rinse out the sample bottle
    D. because the first two quarts always have water present

37. When a rectifier is under automatic control, the device that when operated will shut down and lock out the rectifier is the

    A. a.c. oil circuit breaker, Device 52
    B. a.c. undervoltage relay, Device 27

C. a.c. reclosing relay, Device 79
D. d.c. line circuit breaker, Device 72

38. On a G.E. rectifier, the electrically operated valve (Device 20V) is located in the

    A. cooling water discharge line of the main transformer
    B. cooling water line between the water pump and the heat exchanger
    C. exhaust port of the cylinder block of the rotary vacuum pump
    D. vacuum pipe line between the rotary pump and the receiver tank

39. To measure the load input of a single unit substation, the telemetering equipment is connected to

    A. a current transformer in one phase of the a.c. supply
    B. current transformer in all three phases of the a.c. supply
    C. current and potential transformers in the a.c. supply neutral
    D. a shunt in the main d.c. positive output lead

40. If a supervisory controlled unit, to which the selectors are NOT connected, trips off the line for any reason, the condition will be indicated at system operation board by the lighting of the associated _____ lamps.

    A. white and red
    B. white and green
    C. amber and red
    D. amber and green

## KEY (CORRECT ANSWERS)

| | | | |
|---|---|---|---|
| 1. A | 11. C | 21. D | 31. D |
| 2. A | 12. B | 22. C | 32. C |
| 3. D | 13. B | 23. A | 33. A |
| 4. C | 14. D | 24. A | 34. C |
| 5. C | 15. C | 25. B | 35. B |
| 6. B | 16. A | 26. C | 36. A |
| 7. D | 17. C | 27. A | 37. C |
| 8. B | 18. B | 28. B | 38. D |
| 9. A | 19. D | 29. D | 39. A |
| 10. B | 20. B | 30. B | 40. B |

# TEST 3

DIRECTIONS: Each question or incomplete statement is followed by several suggested answers or completions. Select the one that BEST answers the question or completes the statement. *PRINT THE LETTER OF THE CORRECT ANSWER IN THE SPACE AT THE RIGHT.*

1. Ground indicating lamps are installed to provide an indication of a ground on the substation   1.____

   A. bus potential transformers
   B. main d.c. bus
   C. signal bus
   D. auxiliary d.c. bus

2. A ground relay on a rotary converter would probably operate on the occurrence of a   2.____

   A. ground on the negative bus
   B. ground on the machine frame
   C. breakdown of pedestal insulation
   D. flashover on the rotary

3. When starting a rotary converter from the a.c. side, polarity is checked and if necessary reversed _____ is closed.   3.____

   A. before the field break-up switch
   B. before the *running* switch
   C. after the *running* switch
   D. after the d.c. breaker

4. Rotary converters in manually operated substations are NOT usually provided with automatic devices for protection against   4.____

   A. a.c. over current          B. d.c. reverse current
   C. overspeed                  D. high bearing temperature

5. The solenoids of a field rheostat are energized from the   5.____

   A. 600 volt d.c. auxiliary bus
   B. 600 volt d.c. main bus
   C. bus potential transformers
   D. substation control battery

6. The bell alarm on the signal system will ring when a signal feeder   6.____

   A. circuit breaker trips
   B. current transformer is shorted
   C. transformer becomes overheated
   D. is grounded

7. If an open circuit occurs between two contact points in a rotary converter field rheostat, the rotary   7.____

   A. can be operated if the open coil or grid is short circuited
   B. should be changed over to separate excitation and operated without the field rheostat

31

C. is to be operated at low load with reduced field
D. must be left out of service until the open coil or grid is replaced

8. When a rotary converter is started from the a.c. side, a means is provided to *break up* the shunt field in order to prevent

    A. excessive sparking at the brushes
    B. the rotary from coming up to speed with reversed d.c. polarity
    C. the induction of excessive voltages in the field
    D. the machine from developing excessive speed

9. A ground on the substation a.c. high tension bus would cause the

    A. station d.c. feeder breakers to trip out
    B. rotaries to trip out d.c.
    C. rotaries to trip out a.c.
    D. rotary ground relays to operate

10. Under normal operating procedure and before grounding an a.c. feeder at the substation end, the substation operator must

    A. discharge the cable through a grounded lamp bank
    B. short circuit the three conductors
    C. check that the feeder is grounded at the power station
    D. make sure that no other feeder is grounded

11. For the final fitting of new carbon brushes to the commutator by sandpapering, the preferred method is to draw the sandpaper

    A. in the direction of rotation
    B. opposite to the direction of rotation
    C. rapidly in both directions of rotation
    D. parallel with the commutator bars

12. If it were necessary to take a signal feeder out of service, the FIRST switch or circuit breaker to be opened would be the signal

    A. feeder circuit breaker
    B. transformer circuit breaker
    C. feeder disconnecting switches
    D. transformer disconnecting switches

13. The power factor of a synchronous converter in normal operation will become less lagging as the

    A. load increases              B. load decreases
    C. field current is reduced    D. d.c. bus voltage drops

14. Induction type reverse power relays are installed

    A. at the power station end of the a.c. feeders
    B. at the substation end of the a.c. feeders
    C. on the rotary converter oil circuit breakers
    D. on the rotary converter d.c. positive breakers

15. The emergency alarm circuit through the alarm boxes in the subway is a closed energized circuit. The PRINCIPAL reason for this is to

    A. provide tripping current for the associated breakers
    B. permit testing of the outside boxes at any time
    C. prevent failure, in an emergency, due to an undetected open circuit
    D. avoid false alarms due to accidental open circuits

15._____

16. When a motor-generator set which has been out of service for overhaul and repair is started up, the maximum d.c. voltage generated is 80 volts instead of its rated 120 volts. A possible cause for this condition would be

    A. a reversed direction of rotation
    B. an open circuit in the generator field
    C. a reversal of the generator field connections
    D. the motor running at low speed

16._____

17. The usual method for controlling the d.c. voltage of a rotary converter is by

    A. adjusting the speed
    B. advancing the d.c. brush arms
    C. retarding the d.c. brush arms
    D. varying the shunt field excitation

17._____

18. If the ground indicating lamps show a ground on a substation control battery circuit, the CORRECT procedure would be to

    A. test each cell in the battery until ground is located
    B. open all control switches and keep them open until the ground is cleared
    C. open control switches one at a time to determine which circuit is grounded
    D. ignore the ground as it is not a hazard until a second ground occurs

18._____

19. When starting a rotary converter by means of an induction motor, the speed of the rotary is usually adjusted to synchronism by varying the

    A. rotary converter a.c. voltage
    B. rotary converter field
    C. induction motor input voltage
    D. induction motor rotor resistance

19._____

20. One of the functions of the auxiliary contacts which are closed or opened by the operation of a remote controlled oil switch is to

    A. ground the oil switch when it is open
    B. disconnect the oil switch from the high tension bus
    C. select the appropriate indicating light circuit
    D. permit the switch to be operated manually when necessary

20._____

21. The secondary windings of the potential transformers on the signal feeders are connected to

    A. a low voltage relay
    B. an overload relay
    C. an alarm bell
    D. the red and green indicating lights

21._____

22. When starting a rotary from the d.c. side, the field should be transferred to self excitation

   A. as soon as the unit starts turning
   B. when the unit is up to speed and voltage
   C. after the unit is synchronized
   D. immediately after the positive breaker is closed

23. A quick practical way of determining if the main contacts of an air circuit breaker are making firm uniform contact is to

   A. measure the contact pressure
   B. make an imprint of the contact area with carbon paper
   C. use a feeler gage
   D. measure the voltage drop across the contacts

24. A routine high tension test is to be made from the power station on a substation high tension feeder. At the substation, the operator should erect barriers and

   A. have the conductors clear of ground and of each other
   B. short and ground the three feeder conductors
   C. apply phase identification potentials to the conductor
   D. short the conductors but keep them clear of ground

25. Negative feeders are rarely equipped with switches at the substation because

   A. they are at low potential
   B. excessive arcing would occur
   C. it is seldom necessary to open the circuits
   D. they are not brought up to the switchboard

26. If the signal supply fails in a substation, the signal feeders

   A. are transferred to the a.c. auxiliary bus
   B. are picked up by another substation
   C. are transferred to the d.c. bus
   D. remain *dead* until the supply is restored

27. When cutting in a rotary having a knife switch in series with the positive breaker, the breaker should be closed FIRST

   A. to give the breaker a chance to open freely in case of trouble
   B. to avoid drawing an arc
   C. because it is easier to close the switch than the breaker
   D. to reduce shock hazard

28. In the case of a complete loss of a.c. power to a substation, the operator should immediately open the oil switches on all

   A. a.c. feeders
   B. rotaries
   C. lighting feeders
   D. signal feeders

29. A d.c. positive feeder should be transferred from the substation main to the auxiliary d.c. bus if work is to be done on the

   A. station breaker
   B. track breaker
   C. feeder
   D. main d.c. bus

30. After removing the short and ground from a high voltage feeder which is to be restored to service, the substation operator should IMMEDIATELY

   A. request a phasing test on the feeder
   B. remove all NOT CLEAR tags
   C. test the feeder for grounds with a lamp bank
   D. notify system operation

31. When starting a commutating pole rotary converter from the a.c. side, the d.c. brushes (with the exception of the pilot brushes) should be raised from the commutator

   A. immediately after closing the starting switch
   B. before closing the starting switch
   C. as soon as the d.c. polarity has been checked
   D. after the field break-up switch is closed

32. If the mica insulation between two adjacent commutator segments of a d.c. generator should break down, the result would be

   A. an open circuited armature coil
   B. leakage of armature current to machine frame
   C. a short circuited armature coil
   D. a short circuited field coil

33. A lead sheath relay is intended to operate in case

   A. the d.c. positive feeder breaks down
   B. the d.c. positive feeder goes *dead*
   C. the lead sheath becomes negative to ground
   D. of a reversal of current over the lead sheath

34. Should an accidental ground occur on the negative side of the control battery, the ground detector lamp on the negative side will become dark and the lamp on the positive side will become bright. The reason for this is that there is a permanent ground connection

   A. to the negative side of the battery
   B. to the positive side of the battery
   C. to the midpoint of the battery
   D. between the two lamps

35. If, after a false operation of the emergency alarm, the drop switch (or relay) cannot be restored, the operator should

   A. close the emergency alarm recorder switch
   B. open the single pole switches on the emergency alarm panel before reclosing the feeder breakers
   C. remove the fuses from the feeder breaker trip circuits
   D. leave the feeder breakers open until the drop switch can be restored

36. When starting a rotary converter from the d.c. side, the starting breaker will

    A. trip when the synchronizing plug is pulled out
    B. remain closed until tripped manually
    C. trip automatically when the main d.c. breaker is closed
    D. trip simultaneously with the closing of the oil switch

37. The interpole (commutating) field winding of a rotary converter is USUALLY connected directly in _____ with the _____.

    A. series; armature
    B. series; shunt field
    C. parallel; armature
    D. parallel; shunt field

38. Pitted contact studs on a rotary converter shunt field rheostat should be

    A. smoothed with emery cloth
    B. sandpapered
    C. dressed with a file
    D. resurfaced with solder

39. If the overspeed device on a rotary converter operates, it will open the rotary

    A. control switch
    B. oil switch
    C. positive breaker
    D. negative breaker

40. Starting a rotary converter from the d.c. side does NOT call for the use of a

    A. current limiting resistor
    B. synchroscope
    C. strong shunt field
    D. field reversing switch

## KEY (CORRECT ANSWERS)

| | | | |
|---|---|---|---|
| 1. C | 11. A | 21. A | 31. B |
| 2. D | 12. A | 22. B | 32. C |
| 3. B | 13. B | 23. B | 33. A |
| 4. D | 14. B | 24. A | 34. D |
| 5. D | 15. C | 25. C | 35. B |
| 6. A | 16. D | 26. B | 36. D |
| 7. A | 17. D | 27. A | 37. A |
| 8. C | 18. C | 28. B | 38. C |
| 9. B | 19. B | 29. A | 39. C |
| 10. C | 20. C | 30. D | 40. D |

# EXAMINATION SECTION
## TEST 1

DIRECTIONS: Each question or incomplete statement is followed by several suggested answers or completions. Select the one that BEST answers the question or completes the statement. *PRINT THE LETTER OF THE CORRECT ANSWER IN THE SPACE AT THE RIGHT.*

1. Carbon tetrachloride is no longer recommended for the general cleaning of electrical equipment because of the

    A. limited effects as a cleaner
    B. corrosive effects it has on copper
    C. deteriorating effects on rubber insulation
    D. poisonous effects of the fumes

2. A single-pole single-throw knife switch which is to be installed in a vertical position should be mounted with the hinges at the lower end so that the switch

    A. will open easily
    B. blade will be de-energized when the switch is open
    C. will not close accidentally if the hinges become loose
    D. blade will remain energized when the switch is open

3. If one side of a 120-volt control battery circuit becomes grounded, the voltage on the ground detector lamps will be

    A. 120 volts in one lamp and 0 volts on the other
    B. 60 volts on one lamp and 0 volts on the other
    C. 60 volts on each lamp
    D. 0 volts on each lamp

4. To remove beads of copper from the blade of a knife switch, it is PREFERABLE to use

    A. a coarse stone              B. a fine file
    C. sandpaper                   D. crocus cloth

5. A reel containing an unknown length of cable weighs 340 lbs. If the empty reel weighs 119 lbs. and the cable weighs 0.85 lb. per foot, the number of feet of cable on the reel is

    A. 140        B. 260        C. 400        D. 540

6. Tape and insulating paint should be applied to a rubber insulated braided cable if the

    A. braid shows signs of fraying
    B. cable may be exposed to moisture
    C. copper strands are loose
    D. cable shows signs of overheating

7. In working from an extension ladder, the LEAST important precaution is to

    A. watch for broken rungs
    B. make sure the ladder has no spring or give
    C. avoid tripping on the rope
    D. make sure that the top cannot slip sideways

8. Some transit authority employees receive first aid instructions in order to

   A. be able to provide emergency aid
   B. improve employee morale
   C. decrease the number of accidents
   D. eliminate the need for doctors

9. Before work is started on any power equipment, a hold-off must be obtained. While work is in progress, the hold-off tag should be

   A. in the personal possession of the man in charge of the work
   B. on the desk in full view of the operator having jurisdiction
   C. attached to any part of the equipment worked on
   D. attached to the control switch of the equipment

10. In general, the PRINCIPAL factor which determines the current rating of the fuse that should be installed in a lighting circuit is the

    A. voltage of the circuit
    B. total line current
    C. size of the smallest wire in the circuit
    D. wattage of the individual lamps

11. If one phase of a high tension lighting feeder should break down to ground, the feeder oil switch will be opened by the _____ relay.

    A. reverse current        B. undervoltage
    C. reverse power          D. overload

12. The wire sizes which are arranged in order of their electrical resistance are

    A. 500,000 c..m.;8; 3/0; 2/0
    B. 500,000 c.m.; 3/0; 2/0; 8
    C. 2/0; 3/0; 8; 500,000 c.m.
    D. 8; 2/0; 3/0; 500,000 c.m.

13. When a control system as a whole fails to operate, you should FIRST check the

    A. wiring                 B. controlling devices
    C. source of supply       D. controlled equipment

14. The rules state that employees should not make any statement concerning a transit accident except to proper officials of the transit authority. The PROBABLE reason for this rule is to

    A. prevent lawsuits
    B. avoid conflicting testimony
    C. prevent unofficial statements from being taken as official
    D. give the transit authority officials time to study the case

15. The armature of an a.c. magnetic contactor is composed of laminated iron rather than a solid block in order to

    A. reduce the weight of the armature
    B. produce better contact between the magnet and the armature

C. increase the magnetic strength
D. minimize the heating of the iron

16. A stranded cable of 19 strands, each strand having a diameter of 60 mils, will have a total area, in circular mils, given by the product of

   A. 60 x 19
   B. 60 x 60 x 19
   C. 19 x 19 x 60
   D. 60 x 19 x 22/7

17. Employees of the transit authority are cautioned, as a safety measure, not to use water to extinguish fires involving live electrical equipment. The MAIN reason is that water

   A. may transmit shock to the user
   B. will not extinguish an electrical fire
   C. will turn to vapor and hide the fire
   D. may damage the insulation

18. If copper weighs 0.30 lbs. per cubic inch, a 12 foot section of 2 1/2" x 1/4" copper bus bar would weigh _____ lbs.

   A. 69.2     B. 27.0     C. 2.25     D. 1.875

19. When soldering a lug to a cable, it is considered good practice to FIRST tin the inside of the lug so that the

   A. cable will fit better
   B. solder will not overflow
   C. cable strands will spread easier
   D. solder will adhere more readily

20. In requisitioning insulated wire, it is NOT necessary to specify the

   A. voltage for which it is intended
   B. type of outer covering
   C. thickness of insulation
   D. size of conductors

Questions 21-27.

DIRECTIONS: Questions 21 through 27, inclusive, refer to the following diagram. Disregard the resistance of the two meters and assume that Switch No. 1 is open unless otherwise stated.

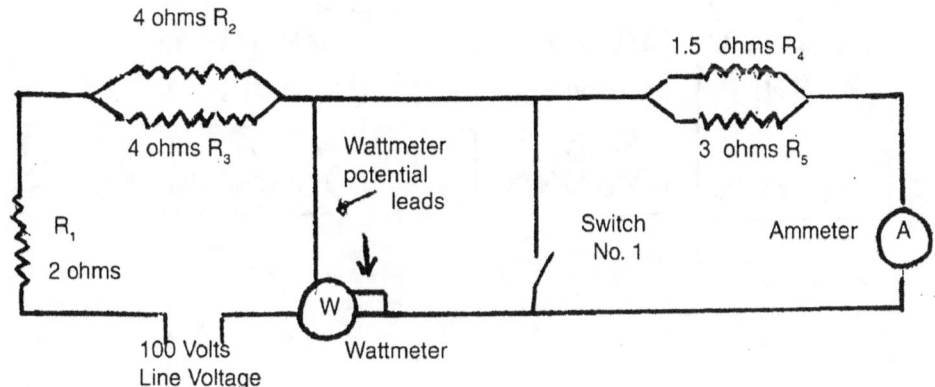

21. The total resistance of the circuit is, in ohms, 21.____
    A. 5   B. 8.5   C. 12.25   D. 14.5

22. The current through each of the 4 ohm resistors is _____ amperes. 22.____
    A. 50   B. 25   C. 20   D. 10

23. If the line voltage is varied, the voltage drop across $R_2$ is always _____ that across $R_1$. 23.____
    A. equal to twice            B. equal to
    C. equal to one-half         D. greater than

24. The wattmeter reading is _____ watts. 24.____
    A. 2,000   B. 1,600   C. 400   D. 0

25. If Switch No. 1 is closed, the current through the ammeter will 25.____
    A. reverse direction         B. increase
    C. be zero                   D. not change in value

26. With Switch No. 1 closed, the wattmeter reading is _____ watts. 26.____
    A. 0   B. 400   C. 2,500   D. 40,000

27. With the Switch No. 1 closed, the total resistance of the circuit is, in ohms, 27.____
    A. 0.8   B. 1.0   C. 4.0   D. 5.0

28. Tabulations have been prepared which list the allowable current carrying capacity of insulated copper wires of various sizes and types of insulation. This allowable current is determined by the 28.____
    A. type of load to be supplied
    B. allowable voltage drop in the circuit
    C. voltage of the source
    D. effect on the insulation caused by the heat generated in the wire

Questions 29-31.

DIRECTIONS: Questions 29 through 31 are to be answered on the basis of the diagram below.

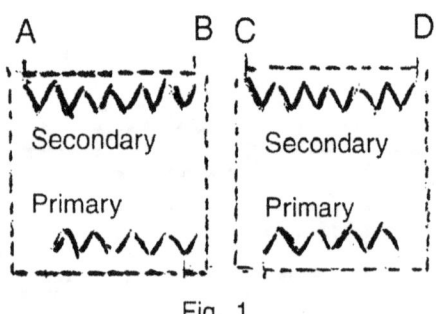
Fig. 1

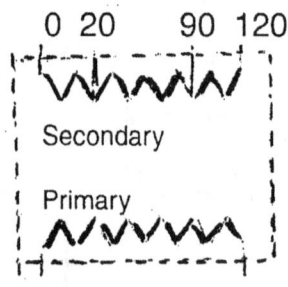
Fig. 2

29. In Figure 1, each single-phase transformer has a ratio of 10/1 and an 11 kv primary winding. To obtain a voltage of 2200 volts from an 11 kv line, the transformers should be connected with the primaries in _____, secondaries in _____.

    A. series; parallel
    B. parallel; series
    C. series; series
    D. parallel; parallel

30. The two transformers in Figure 1 are to operate in parallel. With the primaries connected to an 11 kv source, if secondary terminals B and C are connected together, this connection will be correct for parallel operation of the secondaries if a voltmeter connected between terminals A and D reads _____ volts.

    A. 0
    B. 550
    C. 1100
    D. 2200

31. In Figure 2, the transformer secondary is tapped to give the voltages indicated. Using two connections only and without shorting out any part of the windings, the number of different voltages that may be obtained from the secondary is

    A. 3
    B. 4
    C. 5
    D. 6

32. Failure of a magnetic contactor to close properly would NOT be due to

    A. voltage lower than normal
    B. an open circuited operating coil
    C. voltage higher than normal
    D. excessive mechanical friction

33. Assume that a new type of equipment and controls is to be installed and is to be serviced and operated by you. The BEST and QUICKEST way for you to become familiar with the servicing of this equipment is by FIRST

    A. calling in the manufacturer's agent for instructions
    B. reading textbooks on the general theory of such equipment
    C. making trial disassemblies and reassemblies of some of this equipment
    D. reading the instruction book for this equipment

34. When the presence of water in insulating oil is indicated by dielectric tests, the water is USUALLY removed by having the oil

    A. boiled
    B. distilled
    C. filtered
    D. treated chemically

35. To stop a train in an emergency, a transit employee equipped with only a white flashlight should face the train and wave the light in a

    A. vertical line
    B. horizontal line
    C. vertical circle
    D. forward and backward direction

36. The function of a blow-out coil on an air circuit breaker is to

    A. protect the breaker from high voltage surges
    B. open the breaker in case of an excessive overload
    C. interrupt short circuit currents
    D. extinguish the arc when the breaker opens

37. A standard 110-volt, 5-ampere wattmeter is connected to a single-phase circuit by means of a 5:1 current transformer and a 20:1 potential transformer. If the wattmeter reads 200 watts, the actual power in the main circuit is _____ watts.

   A. 20,000   B. 5,000   C. 1,000   D. 800

38. A 3-phase, 4-wire supply system has a balanced lead of 50 amperes. The current in the neutral wire is _____ amperes.

   A. 150   B. 86.5   C. 50   D. 0

39. The MAIN reason for grounding conduit is to

   A. permit the use of the conduit as a neutral
   B. prevent the conduit from becoming accidentally energized
   C. permit the use of smaller conduit
   D. prevent the conduit from being corroded by electrolysis

40. For maximum output from a rotary converter, the converter should be operated with a power factor

   A. as near to unity as possible
   B. at approximately 80% lagging
   C. as near to zero as possible
   D. at approximately 80% leading

## KEY (CORRECT ANSWERS)

| | | | |
|---|---|---|---|
| 1. D | 11. D | 21. A | 31. D |
| 2. C | 12. B | 22. D | 32. C |
| 3. A | 13. C | 23. B | 33. D |
| 4. B | 14. C | 24. C | 34. C |
| 5. B | 15. D | 25. C | 35. B |
| 6. A | 16. B | 26. A | 36. D |
| 7. B | 17. A | 27. C | 37. A |
| 8. A | 18. B | 28. D | 38. D |
| 9. D | 19. D | 29. B | 39. B |
| 10. C | 20. C | 30. A | 40. A |

# TEST 2

DIRECTIONS: Each question or incomplete statement is followed by several suggested answers or completions. Select the one that BEST answers the question or completes the statement. *PRINT THE LETTER OF THE CORRECT ANSWER IN THE SPACE AT THE RIGHT.*

1. The rectifier will shut down temporarily but will NOT be locked out if    1.____

    A. one phase of the high tension a.c. supply fails
    B. a ground occurs on a feeder breaker (Device 172)
    C. the interphase transformer becomes overheated
    D. three successive overloads occur, each immediately after the closing of the O.C.B.

2. The vacuum pumps on a rectifier are so connected that the    2.____

    A. rotary pump is in series with the mercury pump and between the mercury pump and the rectifier tank
    B. mercury pump is connected to the top of the rectifier tank and the rotary pump is connected to the bottom of the tank
    C. rotary pump is in parallel with the mercury pump
    D. mercury pump is in series with the rotary pump and between the rotary pump and the rectifier tank

3. In a multi-anode rectifier, anode grids are provided to    3.____

    A. give mechanical support to the anode tips
    B. control the rectifier arc
    C. permit convenient access to the anodes
    D. increase the heat radiating surface of the anodes

4. A 36 watt lamp is connected in parallel with the coil of Device 164X on the ground protection circuit to    4.____

    A. keep the circuit closed if the 164X coil became open
    B. give a visual indication of circuit operation
    C. prevent Device 164X from operating instantaneously
    D. increase the current through Device 164X

5. Overtemperature in the mercury pump of a rectifier will cause the operation of Device    5.____

    A. 23V    B. 26TR    C. 27    D. 63V

6. A battery charging motor-generator set which has shut down automatically due to overheated windings resulting from single-phase operation    6.____

    A. will restart when the windings cool off
    B. cannot restart if the battery voltage is too low
    C. will restart when the three-phase power is restored
    D. cannot restart until the thermal relay is reset manually

7. When a rectifier is in normal operation, the mercury pump operates    7.____

    A. only when the vacuum reaches a predetermined value
    B. intermittently

C. only when the rotary pump is not operating
D. continuously

8. If the glow tube is removed from a telemetering transmitter,

    A. the transmitted current will not be smooth
    B. alternating current will pass through the line wires
    C. no current can be transmitted
    D. the line wires will be subjected to excessive voltage

8.____

9. The rectifier holding or auxiliary anodes should fire

    A. when the master contactor (Device 4) is in closed position
    B. only when starting and at light loads
    C. when the rectifier is shut down by remote control
    D. only until the main anodes start firing

9.____

10. In a rectifier, the interphase transformer is connected in

    A. series with and between the cathode and the rectifier breaker
    B. series with and between the negative bus and the power transformer
    C. series with and between the power transformer and the anodes
    D. parallel with the windings of the power transformer

10.____

11. On the closed recirculating cooling system for rectifiers, the water flows from the heat exchanger FIRST to the

    A. water tank
    B. rectifier cathode
    C. rectifier jacket
    D. dome coils

11.____

12. The rectifier water heaters are energized

    A. when the rectifier cooling water temperature is below a set value
    B. when the room temperature falls below a set value
    C. as soon as the rectifier is shut down
    D. continuously when the a.c. control power bus is alive

12.____

13. Raw city water flows to cool the mercury vapor pumps

    A. normally at all times
    B. when the mercury vapor temperature rises
    C. only at high loads
    D. whenever the vapor pressure rises

13.____

14. For pumping the vacuum on a rectifier, a rotary vacuum pump is used in addition to a mercury vacuum pump

    A. to maintain the vacuum if the mercury pump fails
    B. because the mercury pump cannot pump a high vacuum
    C. to avoid overloading the mercury pump
    D. because the mercury pump cannot exhaust directly to the atmosphere

14.____

15. In the system operation office, the indication of a ground protection operation in a single unit station is governed by the

    A. automatic tripping of all the feeder breakers
    B. position of the 186 device
    C. automatic tripping of the rectifier
    D. position of the 164X device

16. Before opening the manual valves on a rectifier, the maintainer should note that the

    A. vacuum gauge (Device 63V) indicates low vacuum
    B. McLeod gauge indicates low vacuum
    C. water circulating pump is operating
    D. tank pressure is within set limits

17. A micron is equal to _____ meter(s).

    A. 10,000
    B. 1,000
    C. 1/1,000 of a
    D. 1/1,000,000 of a

18. The operating element of Device 63V, the vacuum gauge on the rectifier control board, will have a potential to ground of APPROXIMATELY

    A. zero volts at all times
    B. 600 volts at all times
    C. 600 volts when the rectifier is operating and zero when the rectifier is shut down
    D. zero volts when the rectifier is operating and 600 volts when the rectifier is shut down

19. The thermostatically operated rectifier Fulton valve in the GE rectifier cooling system has its thermal element located in the

    A. surge tank
    B. city water supply line
    C. water bled from the rectifier floor coils
    D. heat exchanger

20. A device which is NOT equipped with an operation counter is device number

    A. 4
    B. 51
    C. 52
    D. 72

21. The vacuum tightness of a rectifier is checked by

    A. taking seepage tests
    B. visual inspection of all joints
    C. recording the time of running for the rotary vacuum pump
    D. placing soapy water on joints and seals

22. A rectifier which has been opened to the atmosphere is baked-out by operating the rectifier

    A. at high current but at low voltage
    B. at low current and high voltage
    C. at no load with pumps running continually
    D. and forcing nitrogen gas into it

23. The voltage used to operate the master control relay (Device 103) of a feeder breaker is supplied directly from the _____ bus.

    A. supervisory
    B. control
    C. relay
    D. indication

24. The relief diaphragm is installed on a rectifier power transformer to provide protection against

    A. excessive atmospheric pressure
    B. high cooling water pressure
    C. high vacuum
    D. excessive oil pressure

25. The McLeod vacuum gauge used with mercury arc rectifiers

    A. controls the operation of the vacuum pumps
    B. is manually operated and has no automatic control
    C. acts to shut down the unit in case of poor vacuum
    D. is a combination vacuum indicator and regulator

26. In a GE multi-anode rectifier, the cathode is USUALLY insulated from the main tank by means of

    A. two quartz rings
    B. a porcelain insulator
    C. processed Mycalex
    D. rubber gaskets

27. In an emergency, if a maintainer must de-energize the 600 volt d.c. circuits in a single unit substation, he should

    A. pull the emergency alarm box
    B. turn Device 43 to off position
    C. push the emergency buttons of the ground protection
    D. call the dispatcher's office to trip the circuits

28. Sodium dichromate is added to the rectifier cooling water specifically to

    A. prevent corrosion of the metal
    B. increase the thermal conductivity of the water
    C. permit recirculation of the water
    D. raise the boiling point of the water

29. In stations controlled by load response, the second unit is automatically put in operation when the

    A. operator shuts down the first unit by operating device 205-1
    B. protective device of the third unit opens
    C. station d.c. power output reaches a set value and continues for a definite time
    D. bus voltage falls below a set value

30. In the standard system of automatic switching device function numbers, the numbers 101 to 199, inclusive, are reserved for functions applying to

    A. automatic supervisory equipment used with machines
    B. machine equipment

C. automatic supervisory equipment used with feeders
D. feeder equipment

31. When the power demand requires that two units should run in a station controlled by load response and all protective device circuits are closed, the   31.____

    A. second unit can be prevented from running by operating relay device 243-2
    B. operator by supervisory control cannot prevent the two units from running
    C. second unit can be prevented from running by starting the third unit
    D. second unit can be prevented from running by operating relay device 205-2

32. A rectifier under automatic operation will be shut down and locked out if the   32.____

    A. cooling water pressure falls too low
    B. power transformer becomes overheated
    C. tank pressure becomes excessive
    D. a.c. supply voltage falls too low for safe operation

33. The steel vacuum chamber of a multi-anode rectifier is NOT electrically insulated from the   33.____

    A. arc
    B. ground
    C. main anodes
    D. excitation anodes

34. In the ignitron type rectifier, the igniter is   34.____

    A. immersed in the mercury during the firing period only
    B. kept one-quarter inch above the surface of the mercury
    C. dipped into the mercury then withdrawn to form the arc
    D. immersed in the mercury at all times

35. On the 63V vacuum gauge, the compensating resistance tube is used to   35.____

    A. form an arm of the Wheatstone bridge
    B. compensate for voltage variations
    C. limit the current through the operating element
    D. compensate for temperature variations

36. The rectifier a.c. undervoltage relays are connected   36.____

    A. in series with the potential coil of the a.c. watt-hour meters
    B. to the secondary side of the potential transformers
    C. to the secondary side of the current transformers
    D. in series with the telemetering transformer

37. One advantage of using a.c. auxiliary power instead of the battery power for closing breakers is that   37.____

    A. the closing mechanism requires less maintenance
    B. it is more reliable
    C. less relays are required
    D. a smaller station battery is required

38. The 301 relays in the control room are actuated from the system operation room through selectors joined by the supervisory _____ line.

    A. control
    B. indication
    C. neutral
    D. synchronizing

39. In a multi-unit substation, the failure of a positive 600 volt d.c. feeder to ground with a relatively small fault current will NOT result in

    A. a ground protection indication at the system operation office
    B. the opening of the track breakers in numerical order
    C. the shutting down of all machines
    D. the opening of the feeder breakers in numerical order

40. The device that has to be reset manually after each operation is the

    A. excitation relay on the mercury arc rectifier
    B. a.c. overcurrent relay on the incoming H.T. feeders
    C. thermal relay on a motor-generator charging set
    D. selector synchronizing relay in the control room

---

# KEY (CORRECT ANSWERS)

| | | | | | | | |
|---|---|---|---|---|---|---|---|
| 1. | A | 11. | B | 21. | A | 31. | D |
| 2. | D | 12. | A | 22. | A | 32. | B |
| 3. | B | 13. | A | 23. | C | 33. | A |
| 4. | C | 14. | D | 24. | D | 34. | D |
| 5. | A | 15. | D | 25. | B | 35. | A |
| 6. | D | 16. | B | 26. | B | 36. | B |
| 7. | D | 17. | D | 27. | C | 37. | D |
| 8. | C | 18. | C | 28. | A | 38. | A |
| 9. | A | 19. | C | 29. | C | 39. | C |
| 10. | B | 20. | B | 30. | D | 40. | C |

# TEST 3

DIRECTIONS: Each question or incomplete statement is followed by several suggested answers or completions. Select the one that BEST answers the question or completes the statement. *PRINT THE LETTER OF THE CORRECT ANSWER IN THE SPACE AT THE RIGHT.*

1. Blowers in substations are used to

    A. cool the power transformers
    B. ventilate the substation
    C. cool the rotaries
    D. provide compressed air for blowing out the rotaries

2. A ground relay on a rotary converter will MOST likely operate on the occurrence of a

    A. breakdown of the pedestal insulation
    B. ground on the negative bus
    C. ground on the machine frame
    D. flashover on the rotary

3. The positive d.c. circuit breaker on a rotary converter will NOT trip automatically on

    A. a short circuit at the a.c. rings
    B. excessive starting current
    C. reverse current
    D. overload

4. A microampere is _____ ampere(s).

    A. 1/1,000,000    B. 1/10,000
    C. 1,000          D. 10,000

5. A LIKELY reason for overspeeding of a rotary in service is

    A. an open field
    B. loss of d.c. power at the substation
    C. a decrease in system frequency
    D. loss of a.c. power at the substation

6. The MAIN purpose of the interpoles on a rotary converter is to

    A. maintain constant terminal voltage
    B. provide d.c. load control
    C. improve commutation
    D. prevent hunting

7. On a d.c. shunt generator, the brushes are usually given a forward *lead* from the mechanical neutral to

    A. provide good speed control
    B. reduce brush friction
    C. minimize sparking under load
    D. increase contact area of the brushes

8. If the d.c. control supply to the rotary oil circuit breaker were to fail, the breaker can be tripped by

   A. operating the overload relay by hand
   B. manual operation
   C. operating the overspeed device
   D. actuating the reverse power relay

9. When taking an a.c. high tension feeder out of service, the FIRST switch to be opened is the

   A. disconnecting switch at the power station
   B. oil switch at the power station
   C. disconnecting switch at the substation
   D. oil switch at the substation

10. End play devices are installed on some rotaries

    A. so that the brushes will not wear grooves in the commutator
    B. to prevent the armature from oscillating
    C. so that the bearings will wear evenly
    D. to protect the ends of the shaft

11. A breakdown of the mica insulation between two bars of a commutator on a rotary converter would result in a(n) _____ coil.

    A. open-circuited armature
    B. short-circuited field
    C. short-circuited armature
    D. open-circuited field

12. Operating an emergency alarm box, if only one rotary in the station is on the line, will automatically trip the _____ breaker.

    A. machine positive d.c.      B. feeder
    C. track                      D. machine negative

13. The wye-delta starting of a rotary converter does NOT require the use of a

    A. field break-up switch      B. synchroscope
    C. strong shunt field         D. pilot brushes

14. The drain circuits from cable sheaths to the negative bus should be opened when a substation is shut down to

    A. avoid feedback to the track
    B. prevent excessive current flow over the cable sheaths
    C. prevent grounding the negative bus
    D. isolate the cable sheaths from ground

15. Decreasing the field excitation of a synchronous motor below its normal value when the load is constant will

    A. decrease the speed of the motor
    B. result in a leading power factor

C. increase the speed of the motor
D. result in a lagging power factor

16. The number of pairs of poles on a synchronous converter supplied from an 11 kv volt 25 cycle source and operating at 300 r.p.m. is

    A. 5      B. 6      C. 10      D. 12

16.____

17. The common practice in testing a high tension feeder for grounds is to use a

    A. bank of lamps connected to a d.c. source
    B. glow lamp tester connected to the ground bus
    C. bank of lamps connected to ground
    D. a voltmeter connected to an a.c. source

17.____

18. Series type motors for electrically driven rheostats have a split series field to

    A. be able to carry a heavier load
    B. give a better speed control
    C. prevent excessive motor speed
    D. change the direction of rotation

18.____

19. The purpose of the taps on the winding of a rotary converter power transformer is to provide

    A. potential for the relays
    B. a means of changing the voltage ratio
    C. potential for the synchroscope
    D. a means of changing the input voltage to the transformer

19.____

20. Overcharging a storage battery will NOT cause

    A. excessive gassing      B. water loss
    C. sulphation of the plates      D. overtemperature

20.____

21. If a red or green indicator lamp on the control switch of an oil circuit breaker burns out, it should be replaced IMMEDIATELY to

    A. have a positive indication of the position of the breaker
    B. permit the control switch to operate properly
    C. assure overload protection for the breaker
    D. save the good lamp

21.____

22. While a rotary converter is being started by means of an induction motor on the shaft, the shunt field of the rotary is

    A. completely disconnected      B. separately excited
    C. broken into sections      D. self-excited

22.____

23. The rotary converter positive breakers are provided with a reverse current relay MAINLY to

    A. prevent the closing of the breaker under heavy load
    B. prevent feedback from the d.c. bus if the rotary develops a ground or short circuit
    C. provide protection when the rotary is started from the d.c. side
    D. prevent the closing of the breaker when the bus voltage is low

23.____

24. Before connecting a rotary converter to the d.c. bus, the machine voltage should be adjusted to be APPROXIMATELY _____ than the bus voltage.

    A. one percent higher
    B. five percent higher
    C. one percent lower
    D. five percent lower

25. To prevent the trip coil of a solenoid operated oil switch from being energized when the oil switch is open, the trip coil circuit is USUALLY

    A. connected in series with the green indicating lamp
    B. connected in series with the red indicating lamp
    C. carried through one of the auxiliary contacts of the oil switch
    D. carried through the main contacts of the oil switch

26. An air circuit breaker is adjusted so that the arcing tip will _____ the main contact.

    A. open after
    B. open before
    C. close after
    D. close about the same time as

27. When shutting down a rotary carrying no load, the FIRST step is to trip the

    A. field switch
    B. negative breaker
    C. oil switch
    D. positive breaker

28. The total number of d.c. brush arms on a rotary converter is equal to

    A. half the number of main field poles
    B. twice the number of main field poles
    C. the number of main field poles
    D. the number of main field poles plus two

29. If a d.c. positive feeder were to become grounded just outside of the substation, the station breaker will normally be opened by

    A. reverse current
    B. overload
    C. low voltage
    D. emergency alarm

30. The power factor of a rotary converter in normal operation will change from lag to lead if the

    A. d.c. bus voltage drops
    B. frequency drops
    C. load drops to a low value
    D. load increases in value

31. Slip rings and brushes are provided on wound rotor induction motors to connect the motor to the

    A. field supply circuit
    B. main power supply
    C. overload relays and meters
    D. starting or speed control rheostat

32. In a substation control battery, the pilot cell is the cell

   A. giving the lowest specific gravity reading
   B. selected as a representative for the entire battery
   C. giving the highest specific gravity reading
   D. number one of the battery

33. One method of minimizing the tendency of brushes to wear grooves and ridges in the commutator of a rotary is to

   A. stagger the brushes
   B. undercut the mica
   C. use highly abrasive brushes
   D. use copper leaf brushes

34. A rotary converter is supplied through a bank of three single-phase air-blast transformers. During operation, one of the transformers is found to be considerably hotter than normal while the other two transformers are at normal temperature. A PROBABLE cause for this condition would be that the

   A. dampers are not fully opened on the hot transformer
   B. rotary is overloaded
   C. rotary is operated at a low power factor
   D. cooler transformers are not carrying their share of the load

35. On an emergency alarm circuit, if the gong should sound only once, the PROBABLE cause would be the

   A. accidental opening of the recorder circuit
   B. operation of alarm box having code signal 0-0-1
   C. operation of the test alarm box
   D. accidental opening of the subway closed circuit

36. The purpose of the rotary converter potential transformer is to

   A. energize the potential coil of the reverse power relay
   B. supply power for the oil switch indication lights
   C. provide machine potential for synchronizing
   D. measure the a.c. voltage of the rotary

37. The induction motor mounted on the shaft of a rotary converter for starting purposes has two less poles than the rotary to

   A. keep the starting current at a low value
   B. insure reaching synchronous speed
   C. develop a high starting torque
   D. prevent exceeding synchronous speed

38. The purpose of the two lamps connected in series at the synchroscope is to

   A. indicate if the a.c. bus is alive
   B. provide resistance in series with the synchroscope
   C. illuminate the synchroscope dial
   D. act as a check on the synchroscope

39. An open circuit developing in the coil of a potential relay on a signal feeder will cause    39.____

    A. one ground indicating light to go out
    B. a bell alarm to sound
    C. the signal transformer oil switch to open
    D. the signal feeder oil switch to open

40. The reverse power relays at the substation end of an a.c. high tension feeder have an overcurrent element and a directional element with individual contacts in each relay. To trip the feeder oil switch,    40.____

    A. the directional contacts must be open and the over-current contacts must be closed
    B. both sets of contacts must close
    C. both sets of contacts must open
    D. the overcurrent contacts must be open and the directional contacts must be closed

---

# KEY (CORRECT ANSWERS)

| | | | | | | | |
|---|---|---|---|---|---|---|---|
| 1. | A | 11. | C | 21. | A | 31. | D |
| 2. | D | 12. | B | 22. | D | 32. | B |
| 3. | B | 13. | B | 23. | B | 33. | A |
| 4. | A | 14. | B | 24. | A | 34. | A |
| 5. | D | 15. | D | 25. | C | 35. | D |
| 6. | C | 16. | A | 26. | A | 36. | C |
| 7. | C | 17. | A | 27. | D | 37. | B |
| 8. | B | 18. | D | 28. | C | 38. | D |
| 9. | D | 19. | B | 29. | B | 39. | B |
| 10. | A | 20. | C | 30. | C | 40. | B |

# EXAMINATION SECTION
# TEST 1

DIRECTIONS: Each question or incomplete statement is followed by several suggested answers or completions. Select the one that BEST answers the question or completes the statement. *PRINT THE LETTER OF THE CORRECT ANSWER IN THE SPACE AT THE RIGHT.*

1. According to safety rules, when a maintainer cannot put out a fire in a substation with the fire extinguishing equipment available to him, his NEXT step should be to

    A. notify system operator
    B. call the fire department
    C. vacate the substation
    D. report the situation to his foreman

    1.____

2. The term *number of ohms per volt* commonly refers to the

    A. calibration of an a.c. ammeter
    B. sensitivity of a d.c. voltmeter
    C. constant of an a.c. wattmeter
    D. scale divisions of a d.c. ohmmeter

    2.____

3. Of the following statements concerning wattmeters, the one which is the MOST accurate is that a wattmeter is

    A. used primarily to measure a.c. power
    B. the best instrument to use to measure d.c. power
    C. not used on a.c. circuits when a voltmeter and ammeter are available
    D. as accurate when used to measure d.c. power as it is when used to measure a.c. power

    3.____

4. Of the following, the MAIN factor that determines the capacity of a fuse to be used in a circuit is the

    A. total number of fuses to be used in the circuit
    B. type of equipment the circuit is controlling
    C. maximum current that the power supply can produce
    D. size of the smallest gauge wire in the circuit beyond the fuse

    4.____

5. The terms *Varley Loop* and *Murray Loop* are associated with a method of

    A. pulling cable in manholes
    B. taking cable off cable reels
    C. cleaning cable ducts
    D. locating cable faults

    5.____

6. The MAIN purpose of the emergency alarm system in the authority is to

    A. warn the transit police that an emergency exists
    B. call the fire department in case of a fire on the tracks
    C. cut off power to the contact rail immediately in an emergency
    D. warn anyone who is working on live equipment that the power is on

    6.____

7. A balanced three-phase, three-wire, ungrounded circuit will give the maximum secondary line-to-line voltage when the transformers are connected

   A. △–Y   B. △–△   C. Y–△   D. Y–Y

   7.____

8. A d.c. ammeter registers 10 amps when connected in a circuit. If the two ammeter leads are reversed, the ammeter needle will

   A. register 10 amps
   B. register full scale
   C. vibrate, making it difficult to get an accurate reading
   D. move downscale, making it impossible to get a correct reading

   8.____

Questions 9-16.

DIRECTIONS:  In answering Questions 9 through 16, refer to Column I and Column II below. For each word or phrase listed in Column I, select the item listed in Column II to which it best applies.

COLUMN I

9. Magnetic contactor
10. Rotary vacuum pump
11. Overspeed device
12. Cold seepage test
13. Pilot cell
14. Induction motor
15. Hydrometer
16. Interphase transformer

COLUMN II

A. Mercury-arc rectifiers
B. Rotary converters
C. Batteries
D. Circuit breakers

9.____
10.____
11.____
12.____
13.____
14.____
15.____
16.____

Questions 17-19.

DIRECTIONS:  In answering Questions 17 through 19, refer to Column I and Column II below. For each symbol shown in Column I, select the item listed in Column II to which it BEST applies.

| COLUMN I | COLUMN II | |
|---|---|---|
| 17. [transistor symbol] | A. Diode | 17.____ |
| | B. Transistor | |
| | C. Vacuum tube | |
| | D. Ground | |
| 18. [ground symbol] | | 18.____ |
| 19. [diode symbol] | | 19.____ |

Questions 20-22.

DIRECTIONS: In answering Questions 20 through 22, refer to Column I and Column II below. For each word or words listed in Column I, select the sentence in Column II which BEST describes it.

| COLUMN I | COLUMN II | |
|---|---|---|
| 20. Duct bank | A. It creates an optical illusion of stopping the motion of a moving object. | 20.____ |
| 21. Autotransformer | B. An arrangement of conduit that carries cables | 21.____ |
| 22. Stroboscope | C. A piece of equipment used in testing circuit continuity | 22.____ |
| | D. It has a common winding for its primary and secondary circuits | |

23. An oscilloscope can be used without the addition of any external components as a(n)  23.____
    A. megger      B. ohmmeter
    C. voltmeter      D. wattmeter

24. A meter with a 0-500 volt scale has an accuracy of 2% at full-scale deflection. The maximum error of the meter reading when the pointer indicates 300 volts is *plus* or *minus* _____ volts.  24.____
    A. 2      B. 3      C. 6      D. 10

25. The MAXIMUM rated current-carrying capacity of a resistor marked *5,000 ohms, 200 watts* is _____ amps.  25.____
    A. 0.04      B. 0.20      C. 10      D. 25

## KEY (CORRECT ANSWERS)

| | | | |
|---|---|---|---|
| 1. | A | 11. | B |
| 2. | B | 12. | A |
| 3. | A | 13. | C |
| 4. | D | 14. | B |
| 5. | D | 15. | C |
| 6. | C | 16. | A |
| 7. | A | 17. | B |
| 8. | D | 18. | D |
| 9. | D | 19. | A |
| 10. | A | 20. | B |

21. D
22. A
23. C
24. D
25. B

# TEST 2

DIRECTIONS: Each question or incomplete statement is followed by several suggested answers or completions. Select the one that BEST answers the question or completes the statement. *PRINT THE LETTER OF THE CORRECT ANSWER IN THE SPACE AT THE RIGHT.*

1. If the equivalent resistance of the circuit shown on the right is 25 ohms, the value of R is _____ ohms.

    A. 5
    B. 10
    C. 15
    D. 30

    1._____

2. When a test potential has been removed from a piece of high-voltage equipment, the NEXT step a maintainer should take is to

    A. call system operator
    B. remove all safety grounds
    C. discharge the equipment to ground
    D. remove any *hold-offs* on the equipment

    2._____

3. In an a.c. circuit, *unit power factor* means that the phase relationship between the voltage and the current is

    A. 0°   B. 30°   C. 60°   D. 90°

    3._____

4. In a mercury-arc rectifier cooling system, a selection of rubber hose is used on each side of the

    A. water pump, for flexibility
    B. surge tank, for ease of connection
    C. heat exchanger, for heat insulation
    D. rectifier tank, for electrical insulation

    4._____

5. The MAIN reason for using duct shields around lead sheath cables at the duct edge is to prevent

    A. water from entering the duct
    B. abrasion of the cable sheath
    C. chipping of the duct edges
    D. electrolytic corrosion of the cable

    5._____

6. The abbreviation C.B.M. commonly found on authority drawings refers to a

    A. cable buried in manhole   B. charging battery handset
    C. circuit breaker house      D. current branch hysteresis

    6._____

7. The abbreviation c.p.s. is an acceptable abbreviation for the frequency of an a.c. circuit. Another acceptable abbreviation is

    A. c.p.   B. frcy.   C. f.a.c.   D. Hz.

    7._____

8. As the load on a series motor increases, the motor speed _____ and the _____.

   A. *increases;* field current *increases*
   B. *increases;* field current *decreases*
   C. *decreases;* armature current *increases*
   D. *decreases;* armature current *decreases*

9. Which of the following statements regarding motors and generators is TRUE?

   A. Both a motor and a generator convert electrical energy into mechanical energy.
   B. Both a motor and a generator convert mechanical energy into electrical energy.
   C. A motor converts electrical energy into mechanical energy while a generator converts mechanical energy into electrical energy.
   D. A motor converts mechanical energy into electrical energy while a generator converts electrical energy into mechanical energy.

10. For any given voltage, the current in a series a.c. circuit containing a resistor, a capacitor, and an inductor is at its MAXIMUM when the

    A. circuit is at resonance
    B. impedance of the circuit is at its maximum
    C. reactance of the circuit is at its maximum
    D. capacitor and inductor have the same rating

11. A d.c. voltmeter has an internal resistance of 18,000 ohms and a full-scale deflection of 150 volts. The value of the external resistance that should be connnected in series with this voltmeter so that the voltmeter's range will be extended to 600 volts is _____ ohms.

    A. 4,500   B. 18,000   C. 54,000   D. 72,000

12. In the power department, the abbreviation OCB means

    A. outer copper brush          B. oiled carbon brush
    C. outer cable braid           D. oil circuit breaker

13. Voltage readings taken on six battery cells are 2.21, 2.19, 2.19, 2.17, 2.17, and 2.15. The correction on the voltmeter used is -0.02 volts. The corrected average reading for the six battery cells is _____ volts.

    A. 2.16   B. 2.17   C. 2.18   D. 2.19

14. The expansion and contraction of a cable, which can result in cable failure, is caused MAINLY by

    A. electrolytic corrosion
    B. changing load and temperature conditions
    C. moisture in the air around the cable
    D. the grounding of the cable at its terminal point

15. When the symbol shown to the right appears on an elementary diagram of a d.c. feeder breaker control, it denotes a
    A. circuit breaker
    B. discharged capacitor
    C. contact with a blowout coil
    D. two-wire circuit with a neutral

16. A wattmeter is properly connected to measure the power consumption of an electrical device when the wattmeter's current coil _____ with the device.

    A. and potential coil are both connected in series
    B. and potential coil are both connected in parallel
    C. is connected in series and potential coil is connected in parallel
    D. is connected in parallel and potential coil is connected in series

17. The PRIMARY purpose of the green and red indicating lamps on a high-tension feeder control panel is to indicate whether the

    A. circuit breaker is open or closed
    B. control circuit is open or closed
    C. trip coil is energized or de-energized
    D. closing coil is energized or de-energized

18. A compound is to be heated to a temperature of 90° Centigrade. A maintainer has available to him four Fahrenheit thermometers, each with a different scale. The Fahrenheit thermometer this maintainer should use is the one with a scale ranging from

    A. -40° to 100°
    B. -10° to 150°
    C. 0° to 180°
    D. 100° to 212°

19. A tachometer is an instrument used to

    A. locate cable faults
    B. measure oil viscosity
    C. measure insulation resistance
    D. indicate the speed of a rotating shift

20. If two 1,000 KVA generators are about to be synchronized and the synchroscope is found to be defective, it would still be possible to synchronize them by using the proper circuitry and

    A. two ammeters
    B. two voltmeters
    C. a frequency meter
    D. two ordinary incandescent lights

21. The purpose of a track circuit breaker, when used in connection with a d.c. feeder cable, is to

    A. allow for cable expansion
    B. isolate and remove power from the cable
    C. equalize the voltage between two sections of track
    D. reduce the load through the substation feeder breaker

22. A Wheatstone Bridge is a device used to

    A. locate cable faults
    B. bridge a gap in a field rheostat
    C. measure the value of an unknown resistance
    D. cover live exposed parts when work is done on electrical equipment

23. Which of the following statements about a tool with an exposed sharp edge is TRUE?   23._____
    It

    A. should be carried only in a tool box
    B. should be sharpened each time before it is used
    C. can be used only when a foreman is supervising the man using the tool
    D. can be carried by a maintainer in his pocket if the tool is suitably sheathed

24. According to safety rules, what is the procedure that a maintainer should follow when   24._____
    pulling a fuse in an energized circuit of over 250 volts?

    A. Wear goggles and pull the fuse with his hand covered by a rubber glove
    B. Use an approved fuse puller held in his bare hand and not wear goggles
    C. Pull the fuse with his hand covered by a rubber glove and not wear goggles
    D. Wear goggles and use an approved fuse puller held in his hand covered by a rubber glove

25. Hand blowers should NOT be used to clean high-voltage live equipment because the   25._____
    blowers

    A. stir up the dust around the equipment
    B. are not powerful enough to do the job properly
    C. have a metallic frame that could come in contact with the equipment
    D. do not have an insulated hose of sufficient length to do the job

---

## KEY (CORRECT ANSWERS)

| | | | |
|---|---|---|---|
| 1. | B | 11. | C |
| 2. | C | 12. | D |
| 3. | A | 13. | A |
| 4. | D | 14. | B |
| 5. | B | 15. | C |
| 6. | C | 16. | C |
| 7. | D | 17. | A |
| 8. | C | 18. | D |
| 9. | C | 19. | D |
| 10. | A | 20. | D |

21. B
22. C
23. D
24. D
25. A

---

# TEST 3

DIRECTIONS: Each question or incomplete statement is followed by several suggested answers or completions. Select the one that BEST answers the question or completes the statement. *PRINT THE LETTER OF THE CORRECT ANSWER IN THE SPACE AT THE RIGHT.*

1. Of the following materials, the one that should NOT be used to treat a wood ladder is   1.____

    A. raw linseed oil  
    B. shellac  
    C. spar varnish  
    D. enamel paint

2. Keys, metal key chains or metal clasps for key rings must NOT be worn on the outside of clothing because of the possibility that they might   2.____

    A. be easily lost  
    B. come into contact with live equipment  
    C. get damaged by electric arcing  
    D. interfere with the use of hand tools

3. Operating levers for oil circuit breakers and similar equipment, when not in use, should be   3.____

    A. stood on end and leaned against a wall  
    B. locked up in a storage area  
    C. placed on top of the circuit breaker panel  
    D. kept flat on the floor or on hangers, if provided

4. In the figure shown at the right, the transformer secondary has a continuous winding of 100 total turns with taps at the 20th and 60th turn. Using two different connections at a time, the MAXIMUM number of different voltages that can be obtained from the secondary is   4.____

    A. 4  
    B. 5  
    C. 6  
    D. 8

5. The symbol shown at the right appearing on a wiring diagram represents a   5.____

    A. generator  
    B. rheostat  
    C. wattmeter  
    D. single-pole switch

6. If a maintainer thinks an ambulance should be called to aid a teenager who has been injured in an accident on system property, the maintainer should notify   6.____

    A. a hospital directly  
    B. his immediate superior  
    C. system operator  
    D. his section office

7. Before removing the cover from any manhole in the street, a red flag or lantern must be placed between the manhole and oncoming traffic. Whenever possible, this danger signal should be AT LEAST _____ feet from the manhole.

   A. 5   B. 10   C. 15   D. 20

8. When work is being done in an open manhole, no furnace, hot solder, or hot compound should be placed within _____ feet of the manhole.

   A. 5   B. 10   C. 15   D. 20

9. When a maintainer is on a benchwalk and flagging protection is not provided, he should carry his materials or equipment in

   A. the hand nearest the tracks
   B. the hand nearest the adjacent wall
   C. both hands, distributing the load equally
   D. either hand, depending upon his preference

10. The output d.c. voltage of a battery-charging motor-generator set is usually regulated by adjusting

    A. the speed of the motor
    B. the supply voltage of the motor
    C. a rheostat in series with the battery
    D. a rheostat in the generator field circuit

11. The abbreviation CT, as used in the power department, represents a

    A. current tap
    B. current transformer
    C. circuit terminal
    D. circuit transistor

12. The pilot cell of a storage battery is that cell which

    A. is representative of the entire battery
    B. indicates the highest voltage on overcharge
    C. comes up to full charge before the other cells
    D. indicates the highest voltage with the battery on open-circuit

13. A circuit consists of five standard 36-watt bulbs connected in series across 600 volts. A voltmeter connected across any two adjacent lamps should read _____ volts.

    A. 0   B. 72   C. 240   D. 600

14. The specifications for a particular type of brush call for 2 lbs./sq.in. of contact pressure. For a brush which measures 1" x 1 1/4", the PROPER spring pressure should be MOST NEARLY _____ lbs.

    A. 0.6   B. 1.6   C. 2.0   D. 2.5

15. A watthour meter with a constant of 10 is connected to measure the power output of a particular unit. The reading on the meter is 6876 at a certain time one day and 1244 at the same time the next day. The TOTAL output of this unit for that period of time is _____ kwh.

    A. 18,800   B. 43,680   C. 56,320   D. 81,200

16. Blowout coils are provided on heavy-duty contactors for the purpose of

   A. opening the contactors by remote control
   B. maintaining proper brush pressure on the contactors
   C. tripping the associated breakers in case of a short circuit
   D. extinguishing the electrical arc when the circuit is opened

17. When a rotary converter is started as a d.c. motor, the rotary is brought up to speed

   A. *with* its shunt field self-excited
   B. *with* its shunt field separately excited
   C. *with* the use of a field reversing switch
   D. *without* the use of any starting resistance

18. Which of the following statements concerning the starting of a rotary converter by means of an induction motor is TRUE?
    The inductor motor

   A. is adjusted so that its synchronous speed is less than the rotary speed
   B. is mounted on the shaft of the rotary and has two poles fewer than the rotary
   C. has its speed controlled for synchronization by adjusting the a.c. motor voltage
   D. affects the rotary power factor by a change in the induction motor's shunt field excitation

19. When a rotary converter is started from the a.c. side, all the d.c. brushes, except for one positive and one negative brush, are raised. These two brushes are left in contact with the commutator to

   A. indicate the polarity
   B. provide relay protection
   C. permit control of the speed
   D. maintain unit power factor

20. The relief diaphragm on a rectifier power transformer provides protection against

   A. excessive voltage            B. excessive oil pressure
   C. high vacuum                  D. high water pressure

21. Twelve-phase silicon rectifiers are preferred to single-phase and three-phase silicon rectifiers PRIMARILY because

   A. less maintenance is required
   B. they are smaller and take up less space
   C. a smoother, more even d.c. voltage is obtained
   D. an even number of phases is essential for efficient operation

22. When a rectifier is held off and disconnected from the station positive bus, the power connections to the power transformer should

   A. never be grounded
   B. be connected to ground
   C. be tied to the negative bus
   D. be connected to a low potential safety relay

23. The PRIMARY reason for taking insulation resistance measurements on a machine's windings immediately after the machine is shut down is that, at this time, the insulation is

    A. most likely to break down
    B. relatively free from moisture
    C. most receptive to high voltages
    D. least likely to break dow

24. The PRIMARY function of disconnect switches in a high-voltage circuit is to

    A. close the circuit under load
    B. open the circuit in case of an instantaneous overload
    C. isolate from live buses any equipment that is not in service at this time
    D. maintain continuity of service should the circuit breakers fail to operate

25. A high-tension feeder is ALWAYS phased out before being connected to the bus after

    A. it has been cut and repaired
    B. the substation has *gone out a.c.*
    C. any relay settings have been changed
    D. it has been out of service for an extended period of time

26. Before opening the secondary circuit of an energized current transformer, the secondary windings should be

    A. short-circuited          B. opened
    C. grounded                 D. fused

27. A certain relay is suspected of having some of its windings short-circuited. To verify this, a maintainer should

    A. apply a high potential test and feel the coil for a hot spot
    B. use a test lamp to check the winding for continuity
    C. measure the insulation resistance to the frame of the relay
    D. measure the winding resistance and compare it to the specified resistance

Questions 28-30.

DIRECTIONS: In answering Questions 28 through 30, assume you are assigned to work as a flagman on a particular job.

28. You are NOT responsible for which one of the duties listed below?

    A. Placing and transporting lanterns or flags
    B. Warning the workmen of an approaching train
    C. Giving the required signals to the motorman
    D. Making sure that you are thoroughly acquainted with the job the workmen are doing

29. In what order should the flagging protection be removed upon completion of a job after you have received orders from the employee in charge of the work to do so?

    A. Green flags, yellow flags, portable train stop, red flags
    B. Red flags, yellow flags, green flags, portable train stop

C. Red flags, portable train stop, green flags, yellow flags
D. Portable train stop, red flags, yellow flags, green flags

30. Of the following, which statement is NOT true?  30._____
    A. A red flag or a red light must never be used to give a proceed signal.
    B. A yellow signal color used by you will tell the motorman to resume his normal speed.
    C. In an emergency, any object waved violently by anyone on or near the track is a signal to a motorman to stop.
    D. When you signal a train to stop and the motorman sounds two short blasts of the train's whistle, you can stop signaling even though the train has not stopped.

---

# KEY (CORRECT ANSWERS)

| | | | |
|---|---|---|---|
| 1. | D | 16. | D |
| 2. | B | 17. | B |
| 3. | D | 18. | B |
| 4. | B | 19. | A |
| 5. | B | 20. | B |
| 6. | C | 21. | C |
| 7. | B | 22. | A |
| 8. | A | 23. | B |
| 9. | A | 24. | C |
| 10. | D | 25. | A |
| 11. | B | 26. | A |
| 12. | A | 27. | D |
| 13. | C | 28. | D |
| 14. | D | 29. | D |
| 15. | B | 30. | B |

# EXAMINATION SECTION
## TEST 1

DIRECTIONS: Each question or incomplete statement is followed by several suggested answers or completions. Select the one that BEST answers the question or completes the statement. *PRINT THE LETTER OF THE CORRECT ANSWER IN THE SPACE AT THE RIGHT.*

1. Excessive humming of a magnetic contactor is MOST likely due to

    A. imperfect sealing of the magnet
    B. corroded current carrying contacts
    C. insufficient operating voltage
    D. an opening in the holding coil circuit

    1._____

2. A certain circuit requires a maximum of 10 amperes to operate properly. If a calibrated ammeter in the circuit reads 12 amperes, it is MOST probable that

    A. the ground connection is open
    B. one of the branch circuits is open
    C. a partial short exists somewhere in the circuit
    D. a high resistance connection exists somewhere in the circuit

    2._____

3. When a fire in a substation cannot be put out with the fire extinguishing equipment on hand, the safety rules require you to

    A. call the fire department
    B. shut down the substation immediately
    C. notify system operation at once
    D. ask the nearest substation for assistance

    3._____

4. The sensitivity of a D.C. voltmeter is expressed by the

    A. size of the voltmeter
    B. number of ohms per volt
    C. type of binding posts
    D. number and type of scale divisions

    4._____

5. The word *plan*, when used on a blueprint, indicates a

    A. front elevation view
    B. side elevation view
    C. top view
    D. systematic order of assembly

    5._____

6. If the input to a 2:1 step-down transformer is 10 amperes at 440 volts, the output will be MOST NEARLY _____ amperes at _____ volts.

    A. 5; 220      B. 5; 380      C. 20; 220      D. 20; 880

    6._____

7. Alternating current equipment is usually rated in kva while direct current equipment is rated in kw.
   The reason for this is that

   7._____

A. D.C. equipment is less accurate than A.C. equipment
B. A.C. has a reactive current which also causes heating
C. A.C. equipment uses higher voltages than D.C. equipment
D. in a three-phase A.C. circuit, it is difficult to measure kw

8. A single-phase motor operating at 90% efficiency at full load is connected to a 220-volt source, and takes 10 amperes at 80% power factor.
The power delivered by the motor is APPROXIMATELY _____ watts.

   A. 1,585    B. 1,760    C. 1,955    D. 1,980

9. Five resistors, each having a different current rating, are connected in series. If the resistors are not to be overloaded, the MAXIMUM current permissible in the circuit is determined by the

   A. resistor with the lowest current rating
   B. resistor with the highest current rating
   C. average current rating of the five resistors
   D. sum of the current ratings of the five resistors

10. The device that creates the optical illusion of stopping the motion of a moving object by illuminating it with flashes of light at regular intervals is called a(n)

    A. stroboscope          B. synchroscope
    C. spectroscope         D. oscilloscope

11. Employees are not to walk, stand, or sit in the track area EXCEPT when

    A. very tired
    B. on a work break
    C. waiting for materials to be delivered
    D. necessary for the performance of their duties

12. When necessary to work on energized circuits, all *improperly* insulated tools

    A. should only be used with rubber gloves
    B. should not be used under any circumstances
    C. should not be used except in emergency situations
    D. can be used but should be replaced as soon as possible

13. A megger is an instrument that is used to measure

    A. ampere-hours         B. insulation resistance
    C. frequency            D. illumination

14. When working on the tracks, a bank of lights should be grounded to the

    A. signal rail          B. nearest column
    C. negative return rail D. nearest lighting pipe

15. With respect to ladders, there is nothing wrong with the practice of

    A. placing a ladder in front of an unlocked door
    B. facing a ladder while climbing either up or down
    C. reaching out from a ladder more than an arm's length
    D. skipping over a broken rung when climbing up a ladder

16. The fuse in a certain circuit has blown and is replaced with a fuse of the same rating    16._____
which also blows when the switch is closed.
In this case,

    A. the circuit should be checked
    B. a fuse of higher current rating should be used
    C. a fuse of higher voltage rating should be used
    D. the fuse should be temporarily replaced by a heavy piece of wire

17. A standard knife switch carrying a D.C. load should be opened    17._____

    A. *rapidly,* to avoid blowing the fuse
    B. *rapidly,* to extinguish the arc quickly
    C. *slowly,* to permit the current to *die* slowly
    D. *slowly,* to avoid possible mechanical damage to the switch

Questions 18-25.

    DIRECTIONS: Questions 18 through 25, inclusive, refer to Column I and Column II below. For each abbreviation, word, or phrase listed in Column I, select the item listed in Column II to which it BEST applies. In your answer space, next to the corresponding numbered question space, fill in your selected answer.

| COLUMN I | COLUMN II | |
|---|---|---|
| 18. PILC | A. Wire or cable | 18._____ |
| 19. Cartridge | B. Switch | 19._____ |
| 20. DPDT | C. Battery | 20._____ |
| 21. Hydrometer | D. Fuse or circuit breaker | 21._____ |
| 22. Trip-free | | 22._____ |
| 23. Ampere-hour | | 23._____ |
| 24. Wheatstone Bridge | | 24._____ |
| 25. Circular mil | | 25._____ |

26. The reason for connecting the negative or ground wire before the positive wire when con-   26._____
necting a portable tool to a live 600-volt D.C. circuit is that

    A. the reverse procedure may blow the fuse
    B. there is less danger of accidental shock
    C. electricity flows from positive to negative
    D. less arcing will occur when the connection is made

27. A new maintainer has been assigned to a certain job and told that it must be finished by    27._____
a certain time.
If, after working for some time, he realizes that he cannot finish the job in time, he should

A. notify his foreman immediately
B. skip what he considers minor parts of the job
C. continue working and get as much done as possible
D. take it easy since the job cannot be done in time

28. To prevent a circuit from becoming energized accidentally after opening a switch, a maintainer should

A. block the switch open and tag it
B. ground both terminals of the switch
C. notify his foreman that the switch is open
D. tell all maintainers in the vicinity not to touch the switch

29. When a tool is issued to a maintainer for use on the job, he is NOT held responsible for

A. careful storage of the tool
B. proper and correct use of the tool
C. wear of the tool through normal use
D. reasonable protection of the tool against loss

30. The device often connected across relay contacts to minimize arcing when the contacts open is a

A. spring
B. resistor
C. capacitor
D. transistor

31. If the input to a motor-generator set is 1500 watts and the motor and generator losses total 250 watts, the efficiency of the set is MOST NEARLY

A. 90%   B. 86%   C. 83%   D. 80%

Questions 32-38.

DIRECTIONS: Questions 32 through 38, inclusive, refer to the following circuit. Unless otherwise stated, ALL SWITCHES ARE CLOSED. Neglect the effects of the various meters on the circuit.

NOTE: $R_1 = R_3 = R_4 = 5$ ohms. $R_2 = R_5 = 10$ ohms

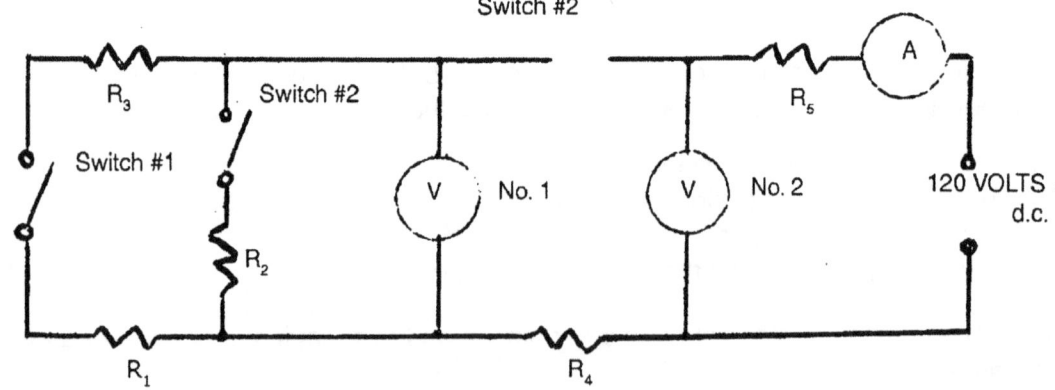

32. The equivalent resistance of the circuit is _____ ohms.

A. 15   B. 20   C. 25   D. 35

33. The current through the ammeter is _____ amperes.  33.____
    A. 6          B. 12         C. 24         D. 30

34. Voltmeter No. 1 indicates _____ volts.  34.____
    A. 120        B. 90         C. 60         D. 30

35. The resistor that dissipates the same amount of power as $R_1$ is  35.____
    A. $R_5$      B. $R_4$      C. $R_3$      D. $R_2$

36. The voltage drop across $R_1$ is _____ volts.  36.____
    A. 75         B. 60         C. 30         D. 15

37. If the two lead wires to the ammeter are reversed, the  37.____
    A. ammeter will indicate zero current
    B. ammeter needle will move backwards
    C. current in the circuit will be reversed
    D. ammeter will continue to indicate properly

38. If Switches No. 1 and 2 are opened, voltmeter No. _____ will indicate _____ volts.  38.____
    A. 2; 0       B. 1; 0       C. 1; 120     D. 2; 60

39. The proper arrangement of the following wire sizes, in order of DECREASING resistance, is  39.____
    A. 1/0; 4/0; 2            B. 4/0; 1/0; 2
    C. 2; 4/0; 1/0            D. 2; 1/0; 4/0

40. Before disconnecting an ammeter from an energized current transformer circuit, the current transformer _____ should be _____.  40.____
    A. primary; shorted       B. secondary; shorted
    C. primary; opened        D. secondary; opened

---

# KEY (CORRECT ANSWERS)

| | | | |
|---|---|---|---|
| 1. A  | 11. D | 21. C | 31. C |
| 2. C  | 12. B | 22. D | 32. B |
| 3. C  | 13. B | 23. C | 33. A |
| 4. B  | 14. C | 24. A | 34. D |
| 5. C  | 15. B | 25. A | 35. C |
| 6. C  | 16. A | 26. B | 36. D |
| 7. B  | 17. B | 27. A | 37. B |
| 8. A  | 18. A | 28. A | 38. C |
| 9. A  | 19. D | 29. C | 39. D |
| 10. A | 20. B | 30. C | 40. B |

# TEST 2

DIRECTIONS: Each question or incomplete statement is followed by several suggested answers or completions. Select the one that BEST answers the question or completes the statement. *PRINT THE LETTER OF THE CORRECT ANSWER IN THE SPACE AT THE RIGHT.*

1. If a self-excited motor-generator comes up to the rated speed but fails to build up generator voltage on the initial start, the FIRST thing to do is to

   A. increase the field resistance
   B. increase the speed of the motor
   C. check the armature insulation resistance
   D. reverse the connections to the shunt field

2. On a certain voltmeter, the same scale is used for three ranges; these are 0-750, 0-300, and 0-15 volts.
   If the scale is marked only for the 0-750 volt range, a scale reading of 300 when the 0-300 volt range is being used corresponds to an ACTUAL voltage of _____ volts.

   A. 15    B. 120    C. 225    D. 300

3. The flow of sufficient current to give positive action to protective lead sheath relays is insured by

   A. proper loading of the feeders
   B. the bonding together of cable lead sheaths
   C. providing more feeders than are required to carry the load
   D. connecting the metering equipment and the protective relays in series

4. A single-phase potential of 240 volts is required for test purposes. A 600-volt source and two identical transformers with 600-volt primary windings and 120-volt secondary windings are available.
   To get the required 240 volts, the transformers should be connected with the primaries in _____, secondaries in _____

   A. parallel; parallel          B. series; series
   C. series; parallel            D. parallel; series

5. The SMALLEST number of single-phase A.C. wattmeters required to measure the total power in a three-phase, 4-wire, unbalanced A.C. circuit is

   A. 1    B. 2    C. 3    D. 4

6. When both fuses and thermal cut-outs are used in a motor circuit, the

   A. fuses should be rated lower than the thermal cut-outs
   B. fuses are used to protect against continuous but not large overloads
   C. thermal cut-outs are used to protect against continuous overloads
   D. thermal cut-outs are used to protect against short circuits in the motor and branch circuits

7. A purpose of the green and red indicating lamps on a high tension feeder control panel is to indicate whether the

A. circuit breaker is opened or closed
B. control circuit is opened or closed
C. trip coil is energized or de-energized
D. closing coil is energized or de-energized

8. A D.C. relay that has its armature magnetically coupled with a permanent magnet is called a _____ relay.

   A. slow acting
   B. quick acting
   C. polarized
   D. rotating disc

9. Of the following devices, the one NOT used to change A.C. to D.C. is a(n)

   A. silicon rectifier
   B. ignitron
   C. motor-generator set
   D. battery

10. A transformer having only one winding is called a(n) _____ transformer.

    A. auto-
    B. potential
    C. constant-current
    D. split-phase

11. In electrical work, the symbol Hz stands for

    A. cycles per second
    B. watts per hour
    C. horsepower
    D. high voltage

12. The 110-volt bus supplying the control power in a substation is often D.C. from storage batteries charged automatically rather than A.C. from a transformer using the A.C. main supply.
    One reason is that the D.C. system

    A. requires less maintenance
    B. is more reliable
    C. requires less power
    D. permits smaller control wires

13. Transistors have replaced vacuum tubes in many electronic applications.
    One reason for this is that transistors

    A. can be used for higher voltages
    B. are larger
    C. cannot become defective
    D. require less power

14. The sum of the following dimensions: 12'11 3/16", 9'8 5/8", 7'3 3/4", 5'2 1/2", and 3'1 1/4" is

    A. 39'5 9/16"   B. 38'3 5/16"   C. 36'2 3/8"   D. 35'1 7/8"

15. Two common transformer voltage ratios used are

    A. 11,000/600 and 208/600
    B. 550/120 and 440/220
    C. 440/600 and 110/440
    D. 120/11,000 and 208/550

16. The MAIN purpose of the carbons in an air circuit breaker is to

    A. prevent flashover
    B. increase breaker capacity
    C. prevent a violent breaker opening
    D. prevent burning of the main contacts

17. If the scale on a drawing is 1/4" to the foot, then a 5/8" measurement would represent an ACTUAL length of

   A. 5'4"   B. 4'8"   C. 2'6"   D. 1'3"

Questions 18-22.

DIRECTIONS: Questions 18 through 22, inclusive, show standard symbols used on drawings. For each symbol, select the word or phrase which BEST describes the symbol.

18.

A. Battery
B. Capacitor
C. Open contact
D. Relay

19.

A. Circuit breaker house
B. Duct cross-section
C. Station platform
D. Street manhole

20.

A. Messenger cable
B. Single pole, double throw switch
C. Earphones
D. Circuit breaker

21.

A. Auxiliary transformer
B. Emergency alarm
C. Diode
D. Substation telephone

22.

A. Cable splice
B. Platform manhole
C. Fuse
D. Control terminal box

23. In a balanced, three-phase, four-wire wye-connected A.C. circuit, the

   A. phase voltage is equal to the line voltage
   B. line current is equal to the phase current
   C. line voltage is equal to twice the phase voltage
   D. current through the neutral is three times the phase current

24. The identifying number F14 on a cable indicates the

    A. negative cable to zone 14
    B. supervisory cable to zone 14
    C. control cable to substation number 14
    D. battery cable to substation number 14

25. An overspeed device on a rotary converter having synchronous speed of 320 rpm is set to operate at 20% overspeed. The device will operate when the speed of the rotary reaches APPROXIMATELY _____ rpm.

    A. 255    B. 300    C. 340    D. 385

26. Each device used in the automatic switching equipment in the power department has been assigned a *device number*.
    The PRIMARY purpose of this numbering system is to

    A. make it more convenient when referring to blueprints
    B. simplify the ordering of replacement parts
    C. indicate the function of the device
    D. prevent confusion between rotary and rectifier equipment

27. The pilot cell of a substation control battery is that cell which

    A. is the middle cell for all batteries
    B. gives the lowest voltage reading on test
    C. gives the highest specific gravity reading on test
    D. is selected as the representative cell for the whole battery

28. In the power department, the voltage level used to differentiate between low voltage and high voltage apparatus is MOST NEARLY _____ volts.

    A. 440    B. 600    C. 700    D. 1000

29. The proper method of determining whether a hand carried carbon dioxide fire extinguisher is undercharged is to weigh it. This type of extinguisher is considered undercharged when the loss of weight is AT LEAST _____ of the charge weight.

    A. 10%    B. 25%    C. 50%    D. 75%

30. In performing a dielectric test of transformer insulating oil, you find, after making the required number of breakdowns on each filling, that the sample you are testing has a mean average breakdown value of 18KV.
    The NEXT step that should be taken is to

    A. notify the section office immediately
    B. take a second sample and test immediately
    C. restore all apparatus to normal operating positions
    D. increase the voltage applied to the sample at the rate of 3,000 volts per second

31. Of the following equipment located in automatic substations, scheduled maintenance is MOST frequently required on the

    A. anode circuit breaker
    B. M-G set
    C. battery panel
    D. rectifier water pump

32. The MAIN consideration which determines whether a protective relay should trip equipment immediately or merely sound an alarm is whether the fault in the equipment

    A. occurs at infrequent intervals
    B. is readily accessible for immediate repairs
    C. can be determined within a reasonable amount of time
    D. is dangerous to the point that it can cause permanent damage to the equipment

33. A rectifier cold seepage test

    A. has no relation to a bake-out in any way
    B. need be made only after a rectifier is baked out
    C. need be made only before a rectifier is baked out
    D. must be performed before a bake-out is started and after the bake-out is completed

34. If there is a discrepancy between the tag on a cable and duct assignment drawing, final positive identification of this cable is BEST made by

    A. spiking the cable
    B. using tracer current
    C. using a D.C. and an A.C. voltmeter
    D. cutting and splicing the cable

35. In the event of a failure to ground in certain substations, one of the purposes of the ground protection is to AUTOMATICALLY

    A. ground the negative bus
    B. de-energize the 600-volt bus
    C. switch the 600 volts D.C. to another substation
    D. switch the high tension feeders to the nearest substation

36. Two tests used to check a silicon diode are the _____ test and the _____ test.

    A. power dissipation; CFM
    B. calibration; surge current
    C. ohmmeter; peak reverse current
    D. thermal current rating; high voltage

37. The newly installed silicon rectifiers are 12-phase rather than single-phase or 3-phase rectifiers. One of the PRINCIPAL reasons for this is that

    A. less routine maintenance is required.
    B. the cathode carries a smaller current
    C. a smoother, more even D.C. voltage is obtained
    D. an even number of phases is essential for good operation

Questions 38-40.

DIRECTIONS: Questions 38 through 40, inclusive, refer to Column I and Column II below. For each method of putting rotary converters into service as listed in Column I, select the sentence in Column II which BEST applies to the particular method

COLUMN I

38. From the A.C. side

39. From the D.C. side

40. By means of special motors

COLUMN II

A. When starting, machine is fully separately excited and when machine is up to speed, shunt field connections are transferred to self-excitation

B. Induction motor is started at 58% of normal voltage supplied by auxiliary step-down transformers through an intervening 440-volt bus

C. Induction motor is coupled directly to rotary shaft and has one less pair of poles than converter

D. In starting, transformer primary is wye (star) connected and when rotary is up to normal speed, transformer connections are switched to delta

38. ____

39. ____

40. ____

# KEY (CORRECT ANSWERS)

| | | | | | | | |
|---|---|---|---|---|---|---|---|
| 1. | D | 11. | A | 21. | C | 31. | D |
| 2. | B | 12. | B | 22. | C | 32. | D |
| 3. | B | 13. | D | 23. | B | 33. | D |
| 4. | D | 14. | B | 24. | B | 34. | B |
| 5. | C | 15. | A | 25. | D | 35. | B |
| 6. | C | 16. | D | 26. | C | 36. | C |
| 7. | A | 17. | C | 27. | D | 37. | C |
| 8. | C | 18. | A | 28. | C | 38. | D |
| 9. | D | 19. | B | 29. | A | 39. | A |
| 10. | A | 20. | D | 30. | B | 40. | C |

# BASIC FUNDAMENTALS OF ELECTRICAL MEASUREMENT

## CONTENTS

| | | Page |
|---|---|---|
| I. | INTRODUCTION TO DC PARAMETERS | 1 |
| II. | AMMETERS, VOLTMETERS, WATTMETERS, OHMMETER, AND OSCILLOSCOPE | 5 |
| III. | AC VOLTAGE AND CURRENT | 8 |
| IV. | MEASUREMENT OF INDUCTANCE AND CAPACITANCE | 10 |
| V. | MEASUREMENT OF FREQUENCY | 12 |
| VI. | ACTIVITIES | 13 |

# BASIC FUNDAMENTALS OF ELECTRICAL MEASUREMENT

I. INTRODUCTION TO DC PARAMETERS

The use of electrical instruments and equipment to make measurements has become a major source of information and data in the complex manufacturing system as it is known today. Sophisticated techniques for electrical measurement were not introduced until the twentieth century, although the study of electrical phenomena dates back to the time of Benjamin Franklin and the American Revolution.

Measurement for electrical parameters is primarily the measurement of voltage, current, resistance, and frequency. However, most electrical measurements require only the measurement of current and voltage. The symbols for the basic electrical measurement parameters are:

I = Current       where    I =

E = Voltage                E =

R = Resistance             R =

F = Frequency

Diagrammatic symbolization of these basic parameters in direct and alternating current are:

$\quad\text{(I)}$ and → = Current

$\quad\text{[|]}$ = Voltage

$\quad\text{-/\!/\!/\!-}$ = Resistance

Voltage is the force that makes current move through the wires of a circuit. Current is the actual movement of electrons through a wire. Resistance is the force that controls the amount of current that can pass through a wire. Frequency in alternating current is the number of cycles occurring in each second of time.

Both voltage and current can be measured with a simple electrical meter which uses magnetism and magnetic characteristics to measure the amount of current that flows. When a meter is connected to an electrical circuit, the flow of current through the coils of the meter creates a magnetic force. This magnetic force is used to move a needle. The amount of voltage, current, and resistance is shown by the position of the needle. The greater the current or voltage, the more the needle moves. To make the measurement easier, a scale is placed behind the needle to measure its movement. This scale is marked to show the value of current on voltage or resistance. The element the meter will measure is determined by the way the meter circuit is constructed and the way the meter is connected to the electrical circuit.

Where a meter is used to measure electrical values, a different circuit is required for each type of measurement. To determine the circuits used, a definition of series and parallel circuits must be made. Resistance in a series circuit is depicted as follows:

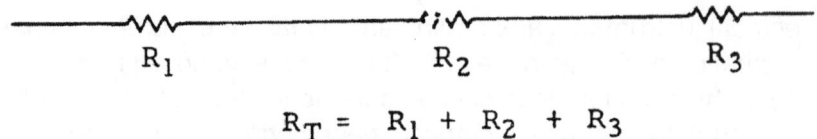

$$R_T = R_1 + R_2 + R_3$$

When two resistors are connected in parallel, they are illustrated as:

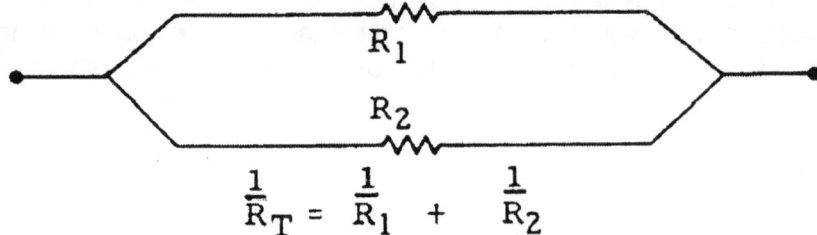

$$\frac{1}{R_T} = \frac{1}{R_1} + \frac{1}{R_2}$$

In a parallel circuit, if either resistor is disconnected, current can still flow through the other resistor. In a series circuit, if either resistor is disconnected, current flow stops because the circuit is broken.

Most circuits have both series and parallel connections and they are called series-parallel circuits. The following figure shows two resistors in series and both in parallel with a third resistor.

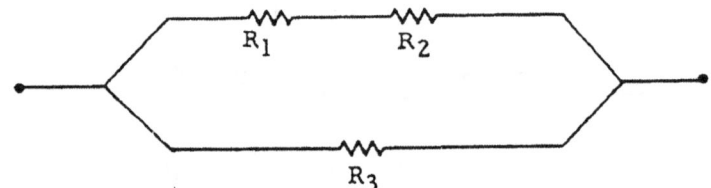

The figure below depicts two resistors in parallel and the parallel resistors in series with a third resistor.

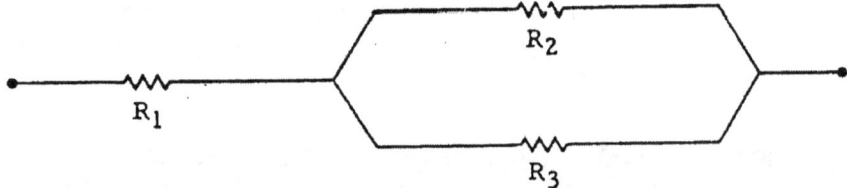

The coil in a meter has some resistance, but more resistance is usually needed. To measure voltage, a large resistance is placed in series with the meter coils as shown below:

For this circuit, the meter is called a voltmeter.

To measure current flow, a small resistance is placed in series with the meter coil and a second small resistor is placed in parallel with the meter and first resistor as shown below:

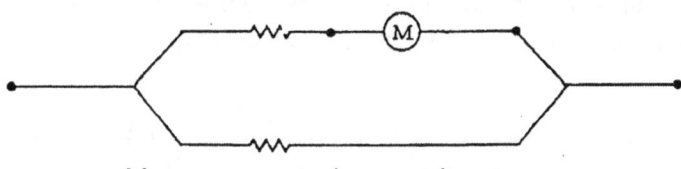

Meter connected as a voltmeter.

A simplified diagram of a D-C moving galvonometer is shown below:

D-C Moving-Coil Galvanometer.

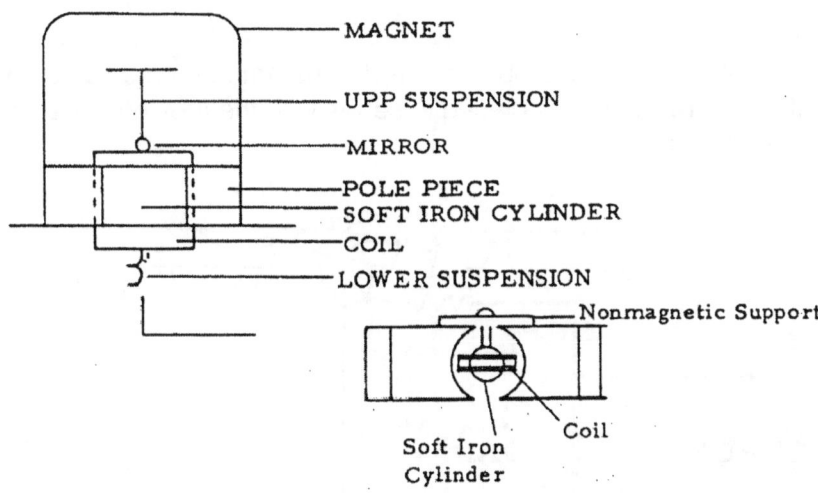

The galvonometer is a basic D'arsonval movement consisting of a stationary permanent magnet and a movable coil with attached mirror and pointer. The use of a pointer permits over-all simplicity in that the use of a light source and a system of mirrors is avoided. However, the use of a pointer introduces the problem of balance, especially if the pointer is long.

II. AMMETERS, VOLTMETERS, WATTMETERS, OHMMETER, AND OSCILLOSCOPE
Ammeter

The basic D'arsonval movement may be used to indicate or measure only very small currents. A simplified diagram of an ammeter is shown below:

The resistance of the shunt is equal to the voltage drop for full-scale deflection divided by the rated current of the shunt.

Current measuring instruments must always be connected in series with a circuit and never in parallel.

Most ammeters indicate the magnitude of the current by being deflected from left to right. If the meter is connected with reversed polarity, it will be deflected backwards, and this action may damage the movement. The proper polarity should be observed in connecting the meter in the circuit. The meter should always be connected so that the electron flow will be into the negative terminal and out of the positive terminal. Common ammeter shunts are illustrated below:

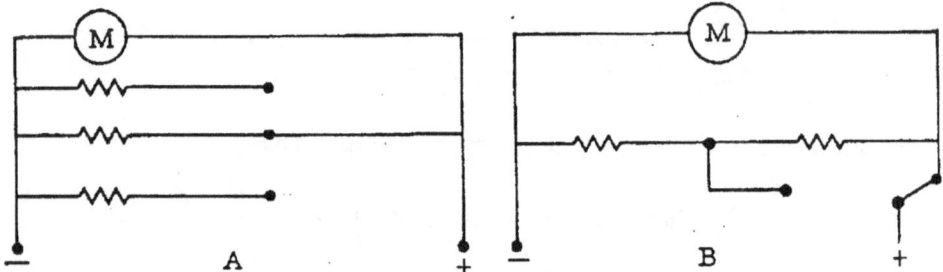

Voltmeter

The D'arsonval meter used as the basic meter for the ammeter may also be used to measure voltage if a high resistance is placed in series with the moving coil of the meter. A simplified voltmeter circuit is:

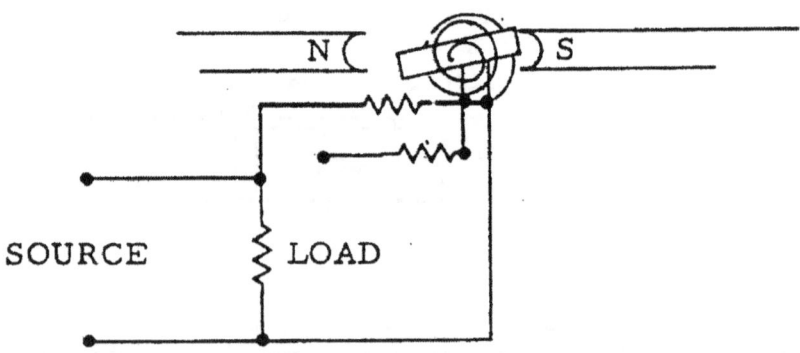

The value of the necessary series resistance is determined by the current required for full-scale deflection of the meter and by the range of voltage to be measured. As an example, assume that the basic meter is to be made into a voltmeter with a full-scale reading of 1 volt. The coil resistance of the basic meter is 100 ohms, and .0001 ampere causes full-scale deflection. The total resistance, R, of the meter coil and the series resistance is:

$R = E/I = 1/.0001 = 10,000$ Ohms
and the series resistance alone is:
$R = 10,000 - 100 = 9,900$ Ohms.

Voltage measuring instruments are connected across (in-parallel with) a circuit.

The function of a voltmeter is to indicate the potential difference between two points in a circuit.

Wattmeter

Electric power is measured by means of a wattmeter. Because electric power is the product of current and voltage,

$$P = I E.$$

A wattmeter must have two elements, one for current and the other for voltage. For this reason, wattmeters are usually of the electrodynamometer type which multiplies the instantaneous current through the load by the instantaneous voltage across the load.

Ohmmeter

The series-type ohmmeter consists essentially of a sensitive milliammeter, a voltage source, and a fixed and a variable resistor all connected in series between the two terminals of the instrument, as shown below:

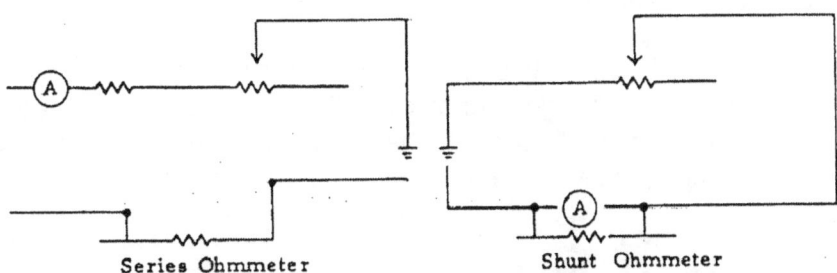

Series Ohmmeter — Shunt Ohmmeter

Before the unknown resistance is measured the test leads are shorted together and the variable resistance is adjusted for full-scale deflection. The point on the meter scale corresponding to full-scale deflection is marked "zero resistance."

The Oscilloscope

Oscilloscopes are used to obtain information about current or voltage in an electrical circuit either to supplement the information given by indicating instruments or to replace the instruments where speed is inadequate. Oscilloscopes permit determination of current and voltage variations that take place very rapidly. These devices are frequently used to obtain qualitative information about a circuit such as current and voltage waves or time relationships between events in a circuit.

This form of measurement also allows determinations of frequency in the form of a graphical illustration. Some examples of the various forms that can be illustrated on an oscilloscope are:

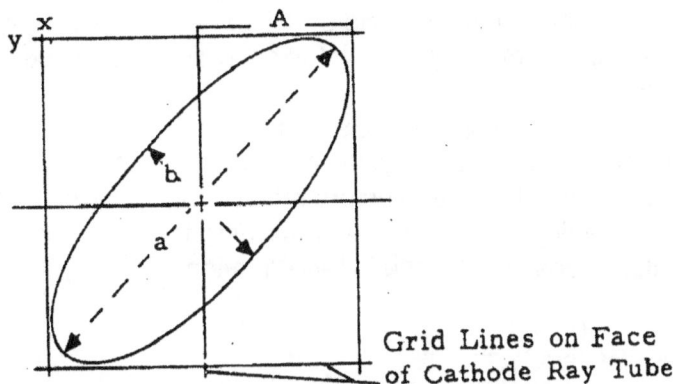

Grid Lines on Face of Cathode Ray Tube

Determination of phase difference of two sinusoidal voltages of same frequency by the pattern on the face of cathode-ray tube.

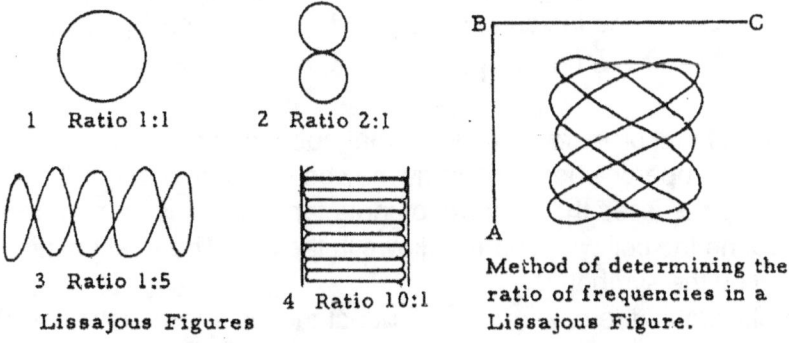

1  Ratio 1:1
2  Ratio 2:1
3  Ratio 1:5
4  Ratio 10:1
Lissajous Figures

Method of determining the ratio of frequencies in a Lissajous Figure.

Lissajous figures are patterns of voltages of different frequencies but related by a simple integral ratio as shown in the preceding figures.

## III. AC VOLTAGE AND CURRENT

An alternating current (AC) consists of electrons that move first in one direction and then in another. The direction of flow changes periodically. Because most of the theory of electric power and communications deals with currents that surge back and forth in a certain manner known as sine-wave variation, the sine-wave is of considerable importance in alternating current. Symbols are:

I or → = Current    ⌇ = Resistance    ⌇⌇ = Inductance
⊖ = Voltage    ⊦ = Capacitance    Z = Impedance

Important characteristics of alternating current are:
1. Cycle - As rotation of a generator continues, the two sides of the loop interchange positions and the generated voltage in each of them is the opposite direction. One complete revolution of the loop results in one cycle of induced AC voltage. This theory is illustrated as shown in the following diagram:

[sine wave diagram, 1 Sec.]

Points 0 to 1 represent one complete cycle of voltage in sine-wave form.
2. Frequency - The number of complete cycles occurring in each second of time. This is symbolized as "F".
3. Period - The time for one complete cycle of the generating force. This is illustrated as 1/f. (For example, the period of a 60-cycle voltage is 1/60 of a second.)
4. Phase Angle - The angle between vectors relative to the positions these vectors represent at any instant of time. This parameter is illustrated as angle 9. One complete cycle of 360 electrical degrees is indicated in the equation:

$e = E\eta \sin \theta$

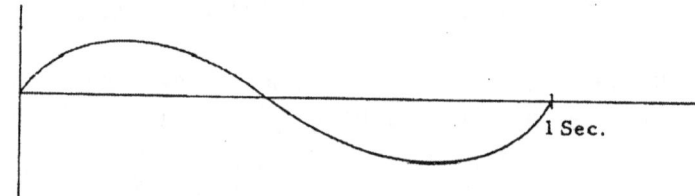

where
- e = instantaneous voltage
- $E\eta$ = maximum voltage
- 0 = the angle in electrical degrees representing the instantaneous position of the rotating vector. Therefore, when 6 = 60', $E\eta$ = 100 volts, e = 100 sin 60° = 86.6 volts.

a. Inductance

Inductance is that property of a circuit that opposes any current change in the circuit. It is also the property whereby energy may be stored in a magnetic field. Therefore, a coil of wire possesses the property of inductance because a magnetic field is established around the coil when current flows in the coil. The relationship of inductance is illustrated by the symbol "L".

In a simple circuit, the relationship of inductance is shown as follows:

In a simple circuit, the relationship of capacitance is *shown* as follows:

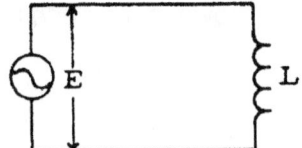

Where E is the applied voltage and L is the inductance.

b. Capacitance

Capacitance is that quality of a circuit that enables energy to be stored in the electric field. In simple form, it has been shown to consist of two parallel metal plates separated by an insulator, called a dielectric.

In a simple circuit, the relationship of capacitance is *shown* as follows:

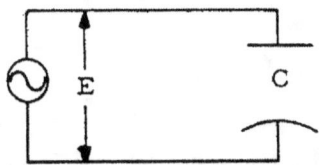

Where E is the applied voltage and C is the capacitance.

## IV. MEASUREMENT OF INDUCTANCE AND CAPACITANCE

Measurements of inductance and capacitance may be made conveniently and accurately by A-C bridge circuits. The simple form of the A-C bridge bears a strong resemblance to the wheatstone bridge. It consists of four arms, a power source furnishes alternating current of the desired frequency and suitable magnitude to the bridge. A four-arm bridge is illustrated in the following diagram:

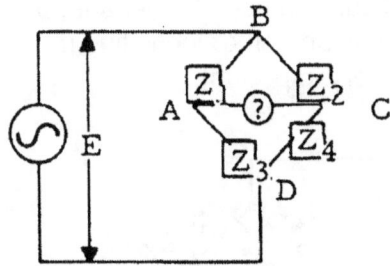

Four arm A-C bridge (using Impedances $Z_x$).

An inductance comparison bridge is similar to form except that the bridge is made up of resistance and inductance relationships. An illustration is as follows:

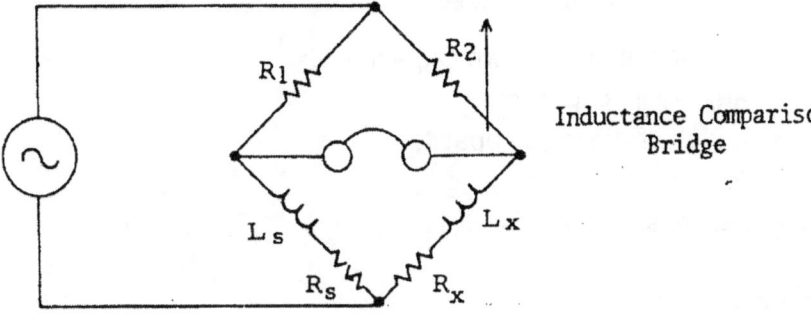

Inductance Comparison Bridge

In the inductance bridge, the relationship shows that the unknown inductance $L_x$ is derived from the equation--

$$L_x = L_s \frac{R_2}{R_1}$$

A capacitance bridge relationship is used to determine an unknown capacitance by comparison to a known capacitance. The relationship is illustrated in the following diagram:

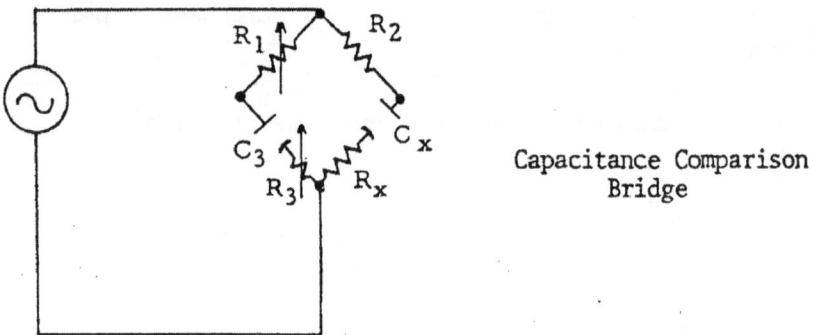

Capacitance Comparison Bridge

Other measurements of inductance and capacitance can be made by using the following bridges:
1. Maxwell Bridge - Permits measurement of inductance in terms of capacitance.
2. Hay Bridge - Differs from the Maxwell Bridge only in having a resistance in series with the standard capacitor, instead of in parallel with it.
3. Owen Bridge - Another circuit for measurement of inductance in terms of a standard capacitor. One arm consists of the standard capacitor only, and an adjacent arm contains a resistance and capacitance in series.
4. Schering Bridge - One of the most important A-C bridges. It is used to measure capacitance in general and in particular, is used to measure properties of insulators, condenser bushings, insulating oil, and other insulating materials. This bridge is illustrated diagrammatically since it is very important.

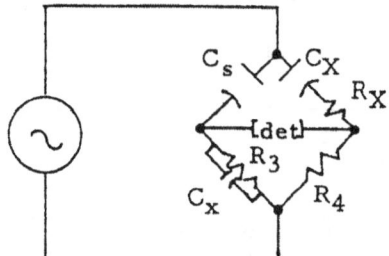

Schering bridge.

$R_x$ = resistance in unknown Capacitor Cx
$C_x$ = adjustable capacitor.
$C_s$ = a high grade mica capacitor.
$C_x$ = air capacitor
The equation is: $C_x = C_s R_3/R_4$

## V. MEASUREMENT OF FREQUENCY

Several types of instruments have been devised to determine frequency. Some of them are: (refer to section on oscilloscope operation and use.)

1. Moving Iron Type - Has a moving element consisting of a soft-iron vane and two crossed stationary coils that are connected with some sort of frequency-discriminating network, so that one coil is stronger at low frequencies and the other at high frequencies.
2. Resonant Electrical Type - Two tuned circuits, one tuned to resonance slightly below the low end of the instrument scale, the other slightly above the high end. These two circuits may be combined with a crossed-coil instrument or an electro-dynamometer to make a frequency meter.
3. Mechanical Resonance Type - A series of reeds fastened to a common base that is flexibly mounted and that carries the armature of an electromagnet whose coil is energized from the A-C line whose frequency is to be measured.
4. Transducer Type - The frequency measuring function is entirely separated from the indicating instrument, which in this case is a simple D-C meter. Two parallel off-resonance circuits are used, one resonant below the instrument range and one above.

VI. ACTIVITIES

1. It is possible to make a simple meter to measure electricity. The materials needed to build a meter are as follows:
   a. One frozen concentrate juice container made of cardboard or a cardboard cylinder of about the same diameter.
   b. One 10 D (penny) nail or a piece of soft steel rod about three inches long and one eighth (1/8) inch diameter welding rod obtained from your teacher.
   c. Enameled wire approximately 28 gauge (American Wire Gauge) about 25 feet. Sources: Industrial Arts or Science teacher, the coil on the back of an old TV picture tube or a hobby store. NOTE: Get the wire from an old TV, unwrap it carefully so that it does not break, kink, or knot up.
   d. One "D" cell battery or any flashlight battery with 1.5 volts (a 9-volt transistor radio battery will not work for this meter).
   e. Two 3x5 note cards.
   f. One small elastic or rubber band.
   g. One flash light bulb.
   h. Masking tape.
   i. Tools: scissors, file, pliers, hacksaw, ruler, and permanent magnet.

   The steps for the construction of the meter are as follows:

   Once the juice container has been washed out, measure two inches along the side of the container, from the open end, and cut this part off to make a cylinder two inches long. This will open the cylinder at both ends. Cut two "V" notches as shown in Figure 4(a), page 16.

Now wrap the wire around the outside of the cylinder. To do this, begin about six inches from the end of the wire and tape the wire to the cylinder 1/8" below one of the "V" notches. Beginning at the notch, wrap the wires neatly around the cylinder each turn next to the other covering approximately one inch of the cylinder. At this point, begin another layer of wire and continue winding on top of the first. Wind this layer in the same direction as the first. Wind layer on layer until sixty-five turns have been made. When it is done, finish at the notch opposite one at which you started and tape the wire in place with a small tab of masking tape. Cut the wire leaving about six inches of lead, save the rest of the wire.

The pointer is made by cutting the head off of the nail. Then mark a point one-third the length from the end of the nail. File both sides of the nail for the two-thirds length until the nail balances at the mark [Figure 4(b), page 16$^4$].

Once this is finished, the short round end of the pointer must be magnetized. To do this, rub one pole of a permanent magnet in one direction over the short round end of the pointer until it is magnetized.

Cut a two-inch piece from the end of a note card. Fold this in half, parallel to the long side to make a "V" shape three inches long and one-inch on a side.

Push the pointer through the center of the card and fasten in place with the elastic, Figure 4(c), page 16 . Position the pointer so that when the card is placed in the "V" notches of the cylinder, it balances and stands up straight.

Attach a 3 x 5 note card to the cylinder so that it is vertical and the pointer can move freely in front of the card. This is a place to mark your readings when you experiment with your meter, Figure 4(d), page 18.

Once the meter is made, you can take measurements. This meter will measure low value of DC (Direct Current) only. <u>CAUTION - DO NOT MEASURE ANY ELECTRICITY OTHER THAN BATTERIES LABELED 1. 5 V DC.</u> These batteries are marked "D", "C", "A", "AA", "AM", "AAAA".

Scrape the insulation off the ends of the wires from the meter coil. Connect each of the meter leads to one of the poles of a "D" cell battery. The meter pointer should move. The position in which it stops should indicate 1.5 volts. Note where this position is.

Clean the varnish insulation from the ends of the wire left over after you wound the meter coil. Connect one end of this to one of the meter leads. Now reconnect the battery with the long length of wire in the meter circuit. Does the meter pointer move as far this time?
Connect a flashlight bulb to the battery so that it lights. Touch the two leads of the meter to the contacts of the bulb. The movement of the pointer to a position on the scale shows the amount of voltage used to get the light to light.

Disconnect your meter and reconnect it so that one end of the battery is connected to the meter and the meter to the bulb, and then the other contact of the bulb to the battery (this is a series circuit). See Figure 5, page 17: The deflection of the meter needle is showing the current used by the light bulb.

The meter constructed is a device much the same as meters made and used in industry. Electrical properties measured are basic to the study and use of electricity. If more information is required on the subject, it is available from several sources.

Among the best sources for information is the nearest library, for both basic and advanced manuals and textbooks. Science teachers in high schools or colleges or graduate engineers, electricians, telephone repairmen, can also help. Many hobby shops and electric supply stores have a selection of basic manuals for sale which provide good background material and a number of experiments with electricity.

In order to build the circuits found in most of these books, a meter movement of greater sensitivity is needed. This can also be purchased at low cost from hobby or electrical supply houses. The meter con-structed from this instruction is only a model to demonstrate how simple electricity is to measure.

2. Visit the electrical laboratory in your school and ask the teacher to demonstrate basic electrical measurements on the meter available. Perhaps the teacher will allow you to practice making simple measurements under close supervision.

3. Arrange a plant visitation at a local electronic or electrical assembly plant. Ask the tour guide to demonstrate the different meters and how they are used in basic measurements.

4. Purchase a Heath Kit or similar meter brand name and assemble as directed. A basic ohmmeter or vacuum tube voltmeter would be a good starting point.

## STEPS FOR CONSTRUCTION OF A METER

Figure 4

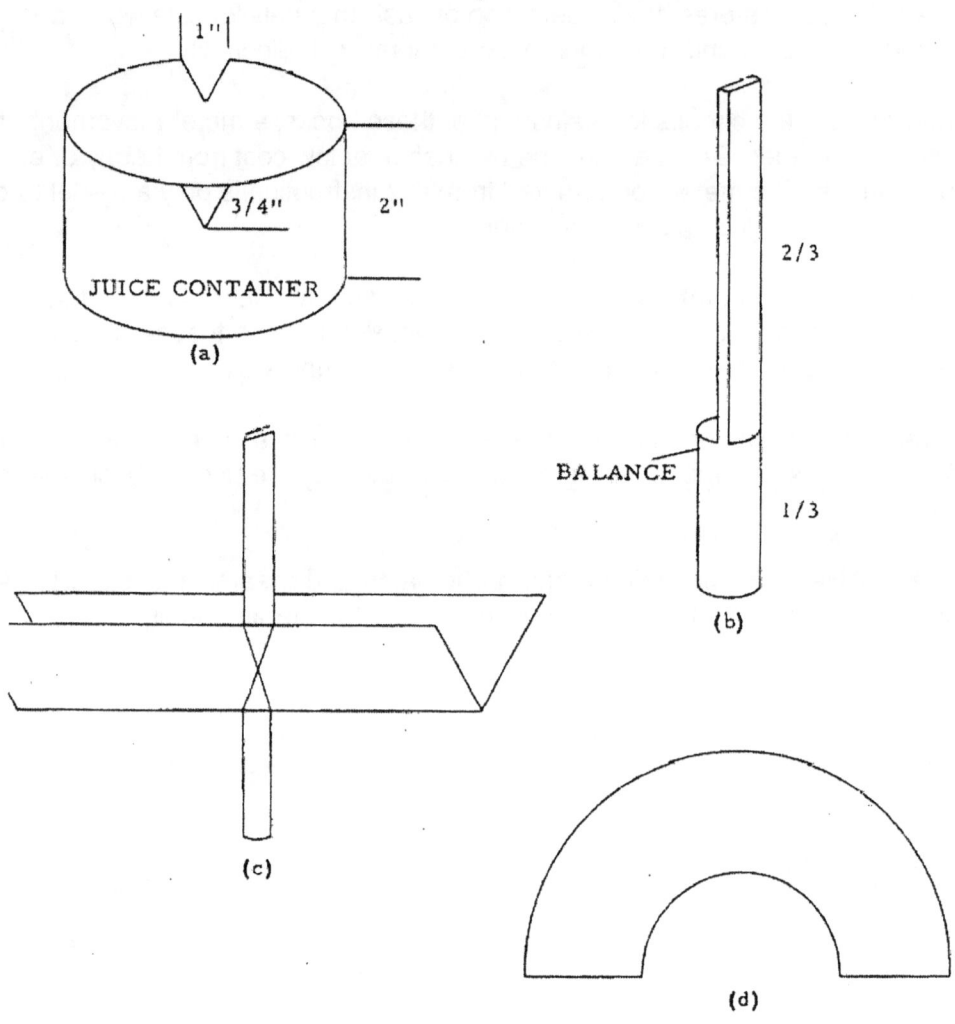

## SERIES CIRCUIT
### Figure 5

SERIES CIRCUIT

Figure 5

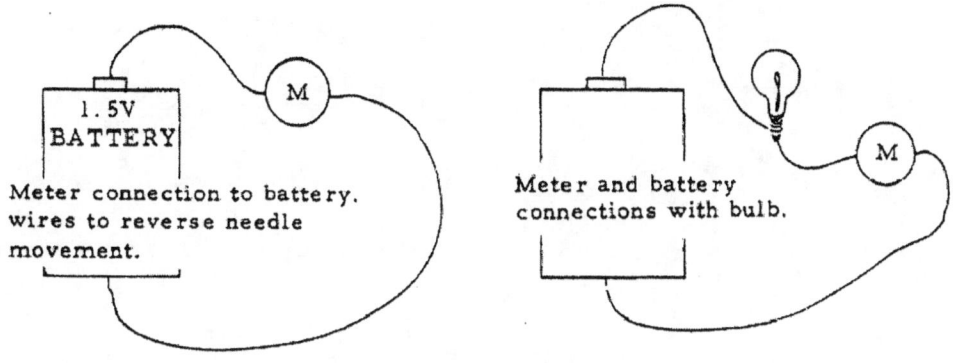

# BASIC FUNDAMENTALS OF BRIDGES IN ELECTRICAL MEASUREMENT

## CONTENTS

| | | Page |
|---|---|---|
| 1. | INTRODUCTION | 1 |
| 2. | WHEATSTONE BRIDGE | 1 |
| 3. | MEASURING CAPACITANCE WITH A BRIDGE | 2 |
| 4. | MEASURING INDUCTANCE WITH A BRIDGE | 4 |
| 5. | PRACTICAL IMPEDANCE BRIDGE | 5 |
| 6. | SUMMARY | 7 |
| 7. | REVIEW QUESTIONS | 9 |

# BASIC FUNDAMENTALS OF BRIDGES IN ELECTRICAL MEASUREMENT

## 1. Introduction

A bridge is a sensitive device used to measure resistance, capacitance, or inductance when great accuracy of measurement is desired. The bridges can be used also for measuring reactance, impedance, and frequency. All bridge circuits include a source of a-c or d-c voltage; an indicating device, usually a sensitive galvanometer or headphones; an adjustable standard, usually a resistor or capacitor; the unknown whose value is to be measured; and a method of determining how much the un- known value differs from the standard.

## 2. Wheatstone Bridge

a. The most common type of bridge used is the *Wheatstone* bridge (fig. 00). The bridge shown is known as the *diamond* arrangement, because the four resistors are shown schematically in the form of a diamond. Resistor $R_x$ is the unknown resistor, $R_a$ and $R_b$ are known as *ratio arms,* and $R_s$ as the *standard arm* of the bridge. $R_a$ and $R_b$ are fixed resistors in the bridge that provide a specific ratio of $R_a/R_b$, and maximum accuracy and sensitivity result when this ratio is 1/1. With the unknown resistor, $R_x$, inserted in the bridge, rheostat $R_s$ is adjusted until the galvanometer reads zero. When this occurs, the voltage drops across $R_a$ and $R_b$ equal the voltage drops across $Rs$ and $R_x$. In A, where $R_a$ equals $R_b$, the ohmic value of $R_s$ (450 ohms) must equal that of $R_x$ for this condition to exist.

b. In B, a slightly different condition exists and the ratio of $R_a/R_b$ is made equal to 200/600 or 1/3. To balance the bridge so that the galvanometer reads zero, the ratio of $R_s/R_x$ must also be 1/3. Since $R_s$ equals 150 ohms, then $R_x$ must equal 450 ohms. This line of reasoning, when put in mathematical form, is shown by the formula,

$$\frac{R_a}{R_b} = \frac{R_s}{R_x}$$

Transposing this equation,

$$R_x = \frac{R_s \times R_b}{R_a} = \frac{150 \times 600}{200} = 450 \text{ ohms.}$$

c. Another Wheatstone bridge circuit, known as a slide-wire bridge, is shown in figure 01. A slide wire, made of a material such as man-ganin and consisting of a single wire divided in 100 equal parts, forms the ratio arm of the bridge. A contact point that can be moved manually along the wire is provided; the re-

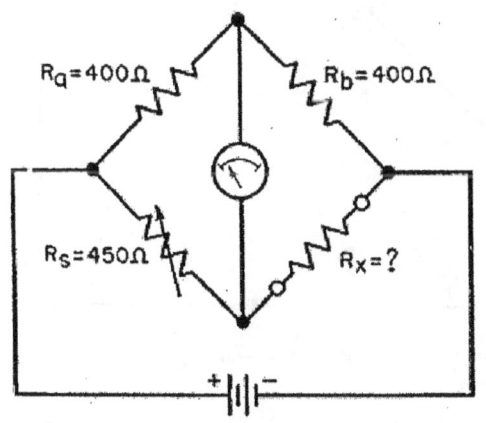 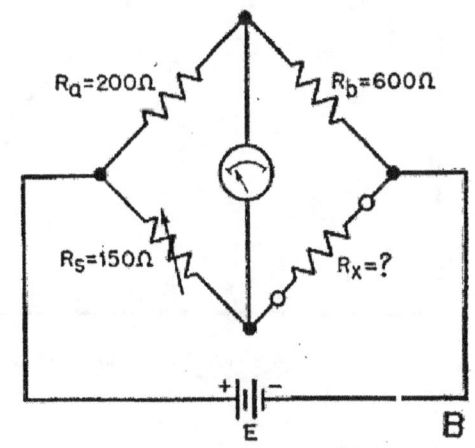

*Figure* 00. *Determining an unknown resistance using diamond arrangement of Wheatstone bridge.*

sistance to the left of the contact point represents $R_a$ and that to the right represents resistor $R_b$. Moving the manually operated contact point along the slide wire varies the $R_a/R_b$ ratio. The standard resistor, $R_s$, has four steps of 1, 10, 100, or 1,000 ohms, making it possible for the bridge to measure different ranges of resistance. An example of the method used to find the value of an unknown resistor can be shown by setting selector switch S to place 10 ohms in the arm. With the contact point in the position shown, scale A gives the value of $R_a$ as 40 ohms, and scale B gives the value of $R_b$ or 60 ohms. The unknown resistor, $R_x$, then can be found by the formula

$$R_x = \frac{R_s \times R_b}{R_a} = \frac{10 \times 60}{40} = 15 \text{ ohms}$$

Nonuniformity of the resistance of the slide wire makes this type of bridge less accurate than the diamond arrangement.

## 3. Measuring Capacitance with a Bridge

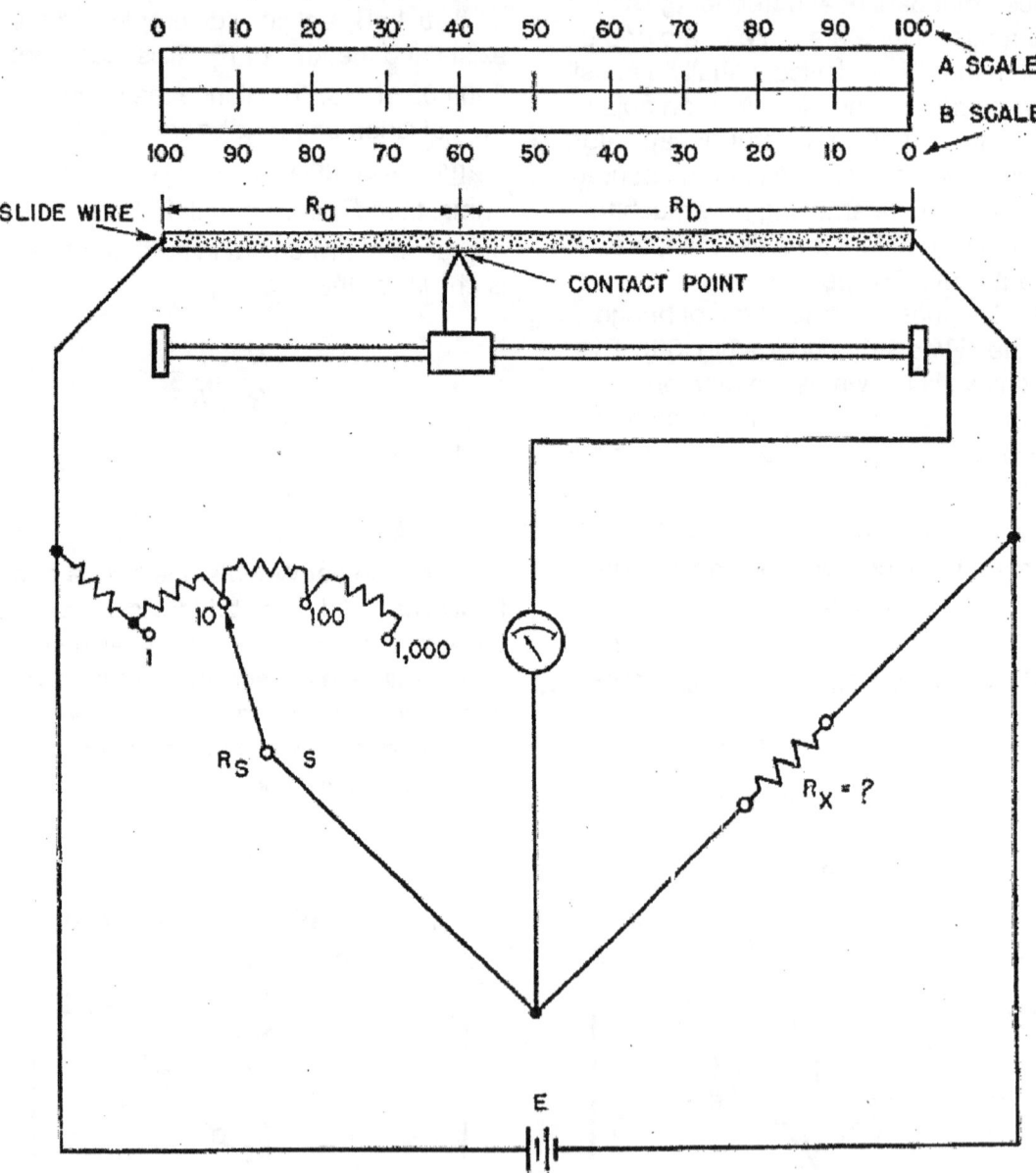

Figure 01. Determining an unknown resistance using slide-wire bridge.

*a.* When measuring an unknown capacitance on a bridge, an a-c source of voltage must be used. This is necessary because the reactance of the unknown capacitor is used to determine its capacitive value. Some typical methods of determining an unknown capacitance are given in figure 102. In the *series-resistance* capacitive bridge, in A, an a-c generator replaces the battery used in resistance measurements. Headphones are used as null indicators instead of a galvanometer, since their pick-up response is dependent on the reactance presented by the unknown capacitance. The ratio arms consist of $R_a$ and $R_b$, with $R_a$ adjustable so that the $R_a/R_b$ ratio can be varied. In the standard arm, a calibrated variable capacitor, $C_s$, is in series with an adjustable resistor $R_s$. Capacitor $C_x$ is the unknown capacitance, and $R_{ex}$ represents the leakage resistance of the capacitor. When the bridge is balanced, the voltage drops across $R^a$, $C_s$, and $R_s$ equal those across $R_b$, $C_x$, and $R_{cx}$. $R_a$ is adjusted to give a specific $R_a/R_b$ ratio, $R_s$ is adjusted to compensate for the effects of $R_{cx}$, and $C_s$ is adjusted to equal $C_x$. $R_s$ and $C_s$ are varied alternately until a zero beat is obtained in the headphones. The dial setting of $C_s$ represents the unknown capacitance. The unknown capacitance can be computed mathematically by the relationship

$$C_x = C_s \times \frac{R_a}{R_b}.$$

6. Another method of determining the unknown capacitance, $C_x$, is illustrated in B. This is known as the *Schering* type of capacitance bridge. The distinguishing feature of this bridge is that the leakage resistance, $R_{cx}$, of the unknown capacitor is compensated for by the adjustable capacitor, $C_a$, which is in parallel with $R_a$. The fixed ratio arm, $R_a$, and the adjustable ratio arm, $R_b$, are connected across the headphones. $C_a$ and the standard calibrated capacitor, $C_s$, are tuned until a zero beat is obtained in the headphones.

*c.* The capacitance of *electrolytic* capacitors, also, can be determined by using a capacitance bridge. However, a polarizing voltage supplied by a battery must be applied to the electrolytic capacitor, as shown in C. Capacitor $C_r$ must be large enough that its reactance at the frequency of the a-c generator is a minimum so that the a-c voltage will be bypassed around the battery. The operation of this type of bridge arrangement is the same as the operation of other types of capacitance bridges.

*d.* When an unknown capacitance is small in value and great accuracy is desired, a *substitution* method is used commonly to determine its value. In this method, the resistors comprising the two ratio arms are made equal in value, and a known capacitor is connected across the terminals that are used to measure the unknown capacitor. The bridge then is balanced by adjusting the standard capacitor, and the reading of the dial setting is noted. The unknown capacitor is connected in parallel with the known capacitor, and the bridge is balanced once more by adjusting the standard capacitor. The

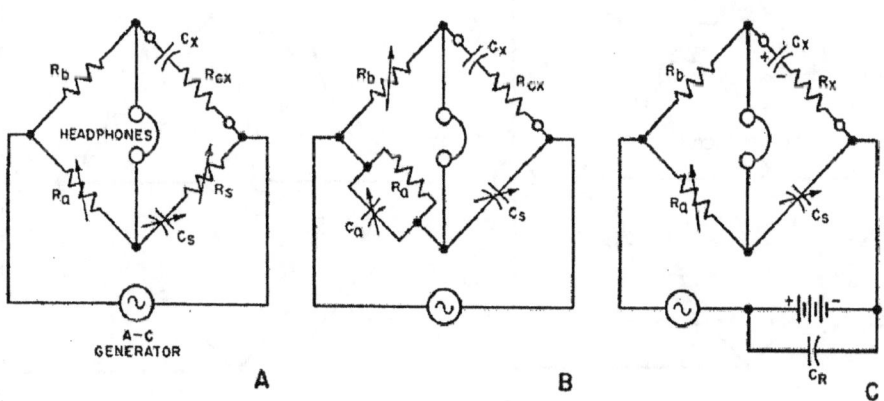

*Figure 02. Typical bridge circuits for determining an unknown capacitance.*

new reading of the dial setting is noted. The *difference* in the two readings is equal to the capacitance of the unknown.

e. The dissipation factor is the ratio of the resistance of a capacitor to its reactance and is a direct check of the capacitors quality. It is equal to

$$D = \frac{R_{cx}}{X_{cx}}, \text{ or } R_{cx} \times 2\pi f c_x$$

where $D$ is the dissipation factor, $R_{cx}$ is the leakage resistance, and $X_{cx}$ the capacitive reactance of the capacitor. The greater the leakage resistance, the greater the dissipation factor, and when the capacitor has a higher dissipation factor than the value specified by the manufacturer, the capacitor should be discarded. In many capacitance bridges, provisions are made to measure the *dissipation, factor* of a capacitor, and many equipments have dials on which it is indicated directly.

### 4. Measuring Inductance with a Bridge

a. An unknown inductance can be determined by using the Maxwell bridge shown in A of figure 03. $R_a$ and $Rb$ are the ratio arms, and both are adjustable to obtain various $R_a/R_b$ ratios. $l_x$ represents the unknown inductance and $R_x$ the resistance of the inductor. The standard resistance, $R_s$, is adjusted to cancel the effects of $R_x$, the standard inductance, and $Ls$ is adjusted to balance the bridge and obtain zero beat in the headphones. The inductance of $L_s$ as read on a calibrated dial equals that of the unknown inductance. The unknown inductance also can be computed by the relationship

$$L_x = \frac{L_s \times R_b}{R_s}.$$

b. Since it is difficult to calibrate accurately a standard variable inductor, variable capacitors often are used as the standard instead of inductors. One type of bridge using a capacitor as its standard (B, fig. 103) is a variation of the Maxwell bridge. The standard capacitor, $C_s$, is adjusted to obtain the proper voltage drops around the circuit, and $Rs$ is adjusted to cancel the effects of $R_x$. The ratio arms, $R_a$ and $R_b$, are used to help balance the bridge and are connected to opposite sides of $L_x$. Dials on the equipment are read to determine directly the inductive value of $L_x$ in henrys, millihenrys, or microhenrys. Inductance also can be directly computed from the relationship

$$L_x = C_s \times R_a \times R_b.$$

c. Another bridge used for inductance meas- urements, known as an Owen bridge, is shown in A of figure 04. As in the Maxwell bridge, $L_x$ is located opposite the standard capacitor, $C_s$, so that a comparison can be made between $C_s$ and $L_x$. A fixed capacitor or a series of capacitors which are switched into the arm, one at a time, can be used to replace $C_s$. The variable capacitor, $C_a$, is used to balance out $R_x$, and $R_a$ and $Rb$ balance the bridge. The mathematical relationship used for determining the unknown

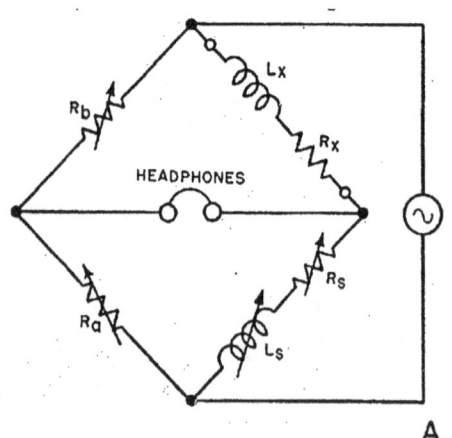
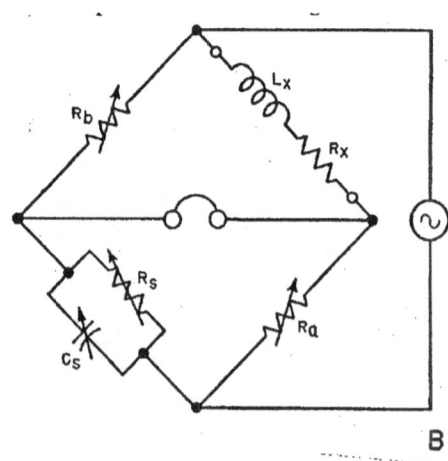

*Figure 03. Methods for determining an unknown inductance, using a bridge circuit.*

inductance in the Owen bridge is identical to that of the Maxwell bridge. Figure 04 shows the similarity between the Hay bridge and the Owen bridge. The standard capacitor, $C_s$, located opposite the unknown inductance, $L_x$, is in series with $R_s$. $Rx$ is balanced by $R_s$, $L_x$ is balanced by $C_s$, and the variable resistors, $Ra$ and $R_b$, complete the balance of the bridge. This type generally is used for measuring inductances having a $Q(X_L/R)$ greater than 10.

    *d.* Just as the dissipation factor is used to measure the quality of a capacitor, *storage factor* sometimes is used to measure the quality of an inductor. Storage factor is defined as the reciprocal of the dissipation factor and is equal to

$$S = \frac{X_L}{R_L}$$

where $X_L$ is the inductive reactance of the coil and $R_L$ the resistance of the inductor. This is identical to the Q (figure of merit) of a coil and it is desirable for an inductance to have a , high storage factor.

### 5. Practical Impedance Bridge
    *a.* SCHEMATIC DIAGRAM.
1. The schematic of a practical impedance bridge used to measure resistance, capacitance, inductance, dissipation factor and storage factor is shown in figure 05. When measuring resistance, the unknown resistor is connected to the RES terminals. When measuring inductance or capacitance, the unknown reactor is connected to the L-C terminals. Switches $S_2$ and $S_3$ are ganged and when positioned as shown (R position), resistance can be measured. Switch $S_1$ determines the amount of resistance in the ratio arms. The resistors of $S_1$–A represent $R_a$ and those of $S_1$_B represent $R_b$ as used in previous bridge explanations.
2. With $S_2$ and $S_3$ in the C position, inductance, dissipation factor, and storage factor can be measured. The L-C terminals are connected, and the RES terminal is disconnected from the bridge. The lower sections of $S_2$ and $S_3$ connect positions, D, DQ, and Q. When in the D position, the upper sections of $S_2$ and $S_3$ are in the C position and the dissipation factor can be measured. The DQ position is used when it is desired to measure storage factor where the Q of the coil is less than 10, and the Q position is used for values of Q greater than 10. When measuring capacitance or dissipation factor, $R_{11}$, $R_{13}$, and $C_1$ are included in the bridge circuit. $R_{11}$ and $R_{13}$ help balance the bridge, and $C_1$ is a d-c blocking capacitor. When measuring inductance or storage factor, $R_{11}$, $R_{12}$, and $C_2$ are included in the bridge circuit. $R_{11}$ is used to balance the bridge for a storage factor greater than 10,

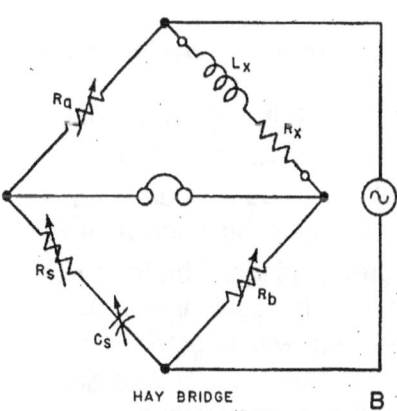

*Figure 04. Owen and Hay bridges used for determining an unknown inductance.*

6

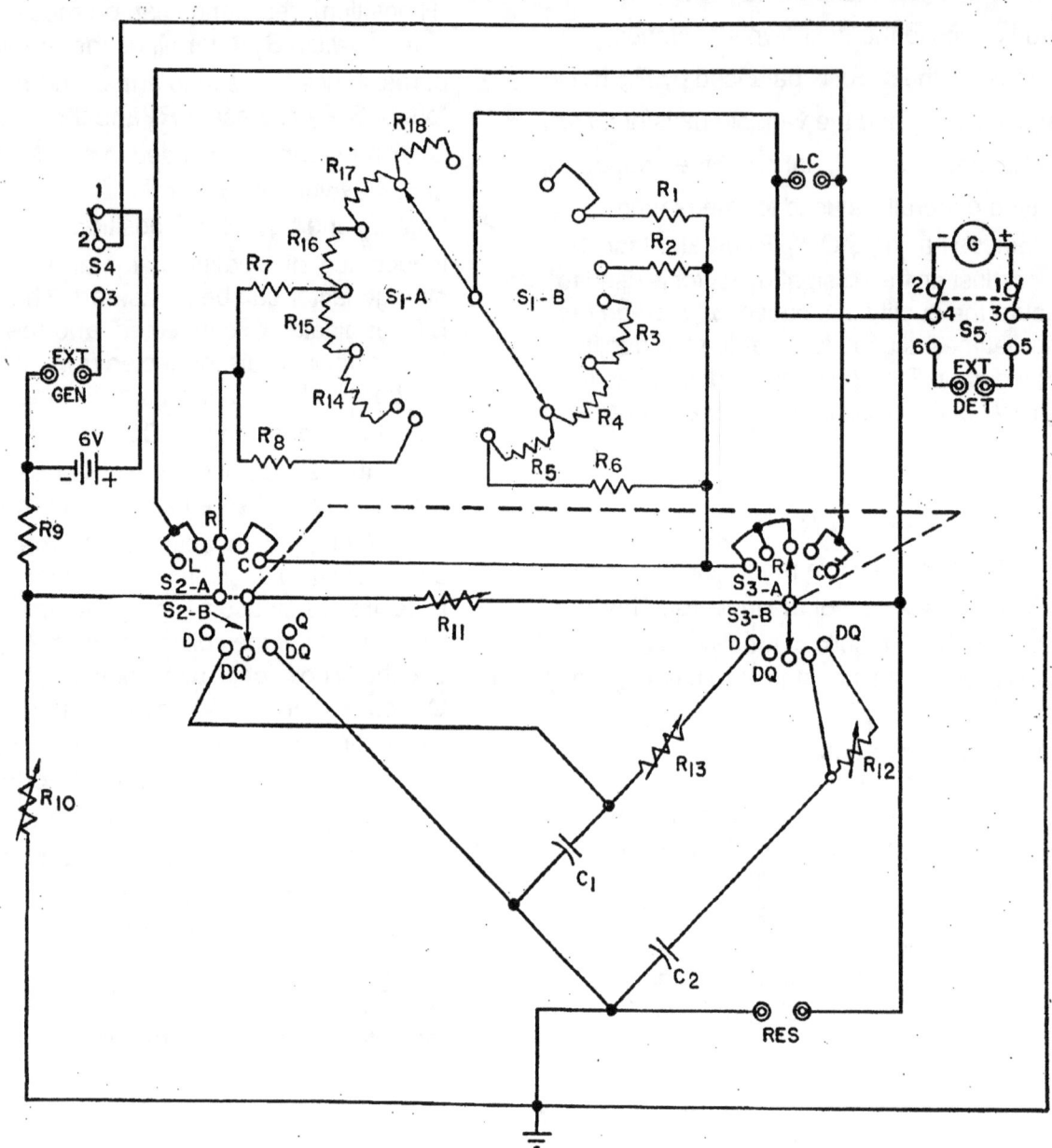

*Figure 05. Schematic of typical practical impedance bridge.*

and $R_{12}$ for a storage factor less than 10. $C_2$ is a d-c blocking capacitor.

3. When resistance is being measured, switch $S_5$ is in the position shown, and the galvanometer is in the bridge circuit. When $S5$ is in positions 5 and 6, headphones can be connected to the EXT DET terminals of the bridge circuit. $S_5$ remains in this position when measuring inductance or capacitance. When measuring resistance, with $S_4$ in the position shown, a 6-volt battery is inserted in the bridge circuit. When $S_4$ is thrown so that the EXT GEN terminals are connected to the bridge instead of the battery, an external a-c source, usually an audio oscillator, can be connected to the bridge. This is the position in which inductance and capacitance are measured. Resistor $R9$ is a current-limiting resistor for the external a-c generator.

*b.* CIRCUIT FOR MEASURING RESISTANCE. If the circuit of figure 05 is used to measure resistance, the conditions shown in the simplified diagram (fig. .06) exist. With switches $S_2$ and $S_3$ in the $R$ positions and $S_1$–$A$ as shown, the $R_a$ ratio arm consists of $R_7$, $R_{16}$, and $R_{17}$. Switch $S_1$–$B$ puts $R_5$ and $R_6$ in the ratio arm $R_{b'}$. With $S_5$ in the position shown, the galvanometer also is in the bridge and the 6-volt battery is connected in the circuit. The unknown resistor, $R_x$, is inserted between the RES terminals, and the calibrated resistor, $R_{10}$ (the standard) is adjusted to balance the bridge. The ohmic value of the unknown resistor is read on the panel of the bridge equipment. Its reading is dependent upon the ohmic values of the two ratio arms and $R_{10}$.

*c.* MAXWELL BRIDGE. The Maxwell bridge circuit arrangement of figure 05 can be used also to measure inductance and storage factor (fig. 07). With $S_2$ and $S_s$ in the L, DQ positions, headphones are connected to the EXT DET terminals, and an audio oscillator is connected to the EXT GEN terminals. The unknown inductor, $L_x$, then is connected to the L-C terminals and $R_{10}$ and $R_{11}$ are adjusted to balance the bridge (minimum indication in the headphones). Resistor $R_x$ represents the d-c resistance of the unknown inductor. Inductance and storage factor are read directly from dials on the bridge equipment.

*d.* HAY BRIDGE. The circuit shown in figure 105 can be connected as a Hay bridge to measure inductance and storage factor (fig..08). The Hay bridge is used to measure storage factors greater than 10. The arrangement of all the switches in the Hay bridge is the same as those for the Maxwell bridge with the exception of $S_2$ and $S_3$. These switches are arranged so that their lower sections are connected to the Q position, their upper sections remaining in the L position. Resistor $R_{12}$ in series with capacitor $C_1$ is the standard arm of the bridge. The remainder of the Hay bridge is identical to the Maxwell bridge arrangement.

*e.* CIRCUIT FOR MEASURING CAPACITANCE. The circuit of figure 05 also can be arranged (fig. 09) to measure an unknown capacitor and dissipation factor. Switches $S_2$ and $S_3$ are arranged so that their upper sections are in the C position and their lower sections are in the D position. This causes $C_1$ to be in series with $R_{13}$ in the standard arm. $R_5$ and $R_6$ become the $R_b$ ratio arm. $C_x$ represents the capacitance to be measured, and $R_x$ the d-c resistance of the capacitor. The bridge is balanced by adjusting $R_{10}$ and $R_{13}$. A minimum indication is heard in the headphones, and capacitance, or dissipation factor, is read directly on the panel of the bridge.

## 6. Summary

*a.* A bridge is a sensitive device which is used to measure an unknown resistance, capacitance, inductance, or reactance.

*b.* The most common bridge used to measure an unknown resistance is the Wheatstone bridge.

*c.* The mathematical relationship for determining an unknown resistance in a bridge circuit is

$$R_x = \frac{R_s \times R_b}{R_a}.$$

*d.* A slide-wire Wheatstone bridge uses a single piece of high-resistance wire as the $R_a$ and $R_b$ ratio arms.

*e.* When measuring an unknown capacitance, an a-c generator and headphones are used instead of a battery and galvanometer as in a Wheatstone bridge.

*f.* The mathematical relationship for determining an unknown capacitor in a bridge circuit is

$$C_x = C_s \times \frac{R_a}{R_b}.$$

*g.* Dissipation factor determines the leakage resistance of a capacitor and is equal to the leakage resistance divided by the reactance of the capacitor, or $R_{cx} \times 2\pi f c_x$

*h.* Inductance bridges often use variable capacitors instead of variable inductors as the standard because they are easier to calibrate.

*i.* The mathematical relationship for determining an unknown inductor in a bridge circuit is

$$L_x = C_s \times R_a \times R_b.$$

*j.* Storage factor determines the worth of an inductor and is equal to its reactance divided by its d-c resistance.

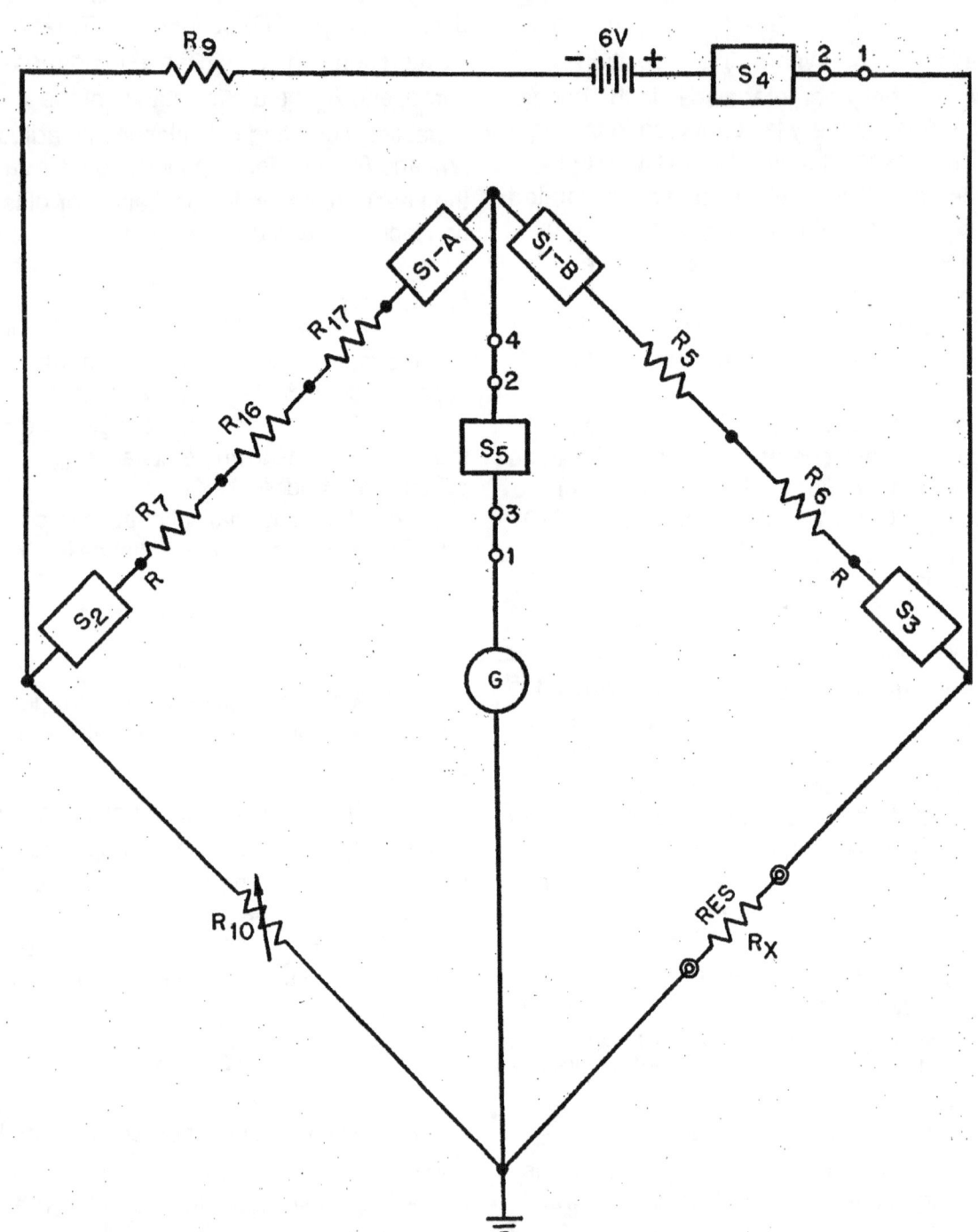

*Figure 06. Circuit for measuring resistance.*

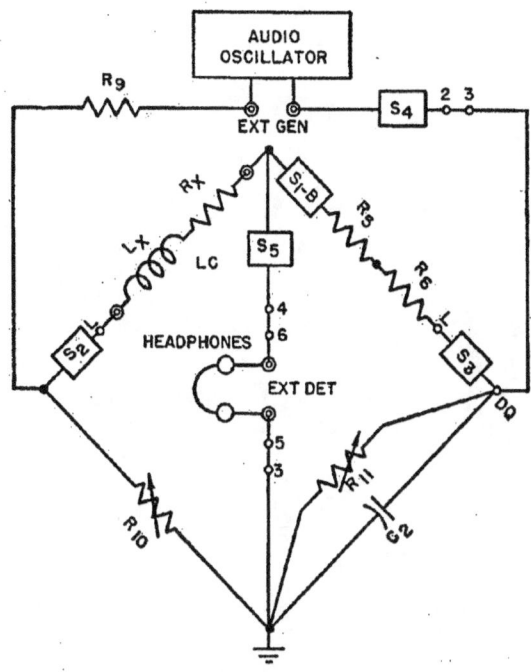

*Figure 07. Maxwell bridge circuit for measuring inductance and storage factor.*

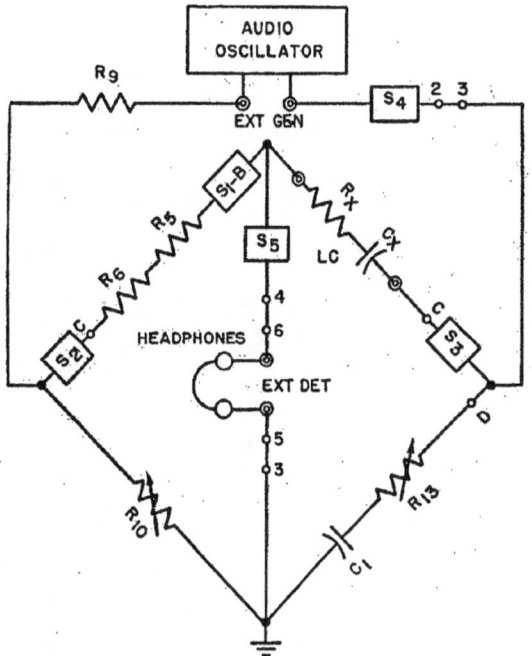

*Figure 09. Circuit for measuring capacitance and dissipation factor.*

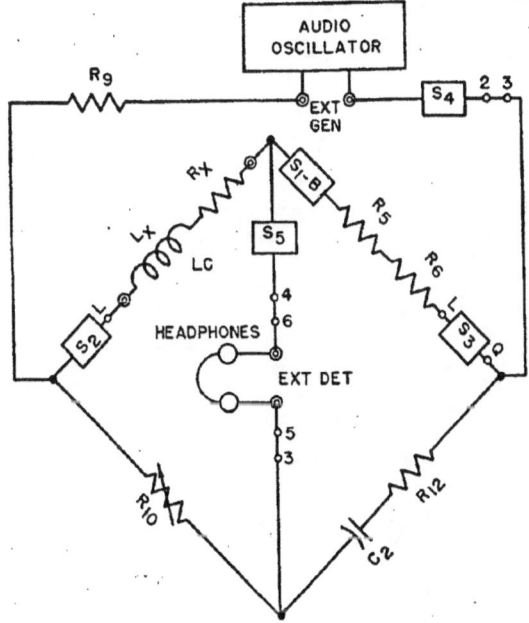

*Figure 08. Hay bridge circuit for measuring inductance and storage factor.*

## 7. Review Questions

a. Define a bridge circuit.

b. Can a Wheatstone bridge be used to measure an unknown reactance?

c. Why is it desirable to have the $R_b/R_a$ ratio in a Wheatstone bridge equal to 1 ?

d. What is the distinguishing characteristic of a slide-wire type Wheatstone bridge?

e. Why are a-c generators and headphones used in reactive bridge circuits instead of batteries and galvanometers ?

f. What changes must be made in a capacitive bridge circuit when measuring an electrolytic capacitor?

g. Explain the difference between dissipation factor and storage factor.

h. If capacitive bridges use capacitors as the standard, then why do not inductive bridges use inductors as the standard?

i. What are the mathematical relationships for determining an unknown resistor, capacitor, and inductor in a bridge circuit?

j. What is a storage factor?

# ELECTRICAL TERMS AND FORMULAS

## CONTENTS

|   | Page |
|---|---|
| **TERMS** | 1 |
|    Agonic ...... Dielectric | 1 |
|    Diode ...... Lead | 2 |
|    Line of Force ...... Resistor | 3 |
|    Retentivity ...... Wattmeter | 4 |
| **FORMULAS** | 4 |
|    Ohm's Law for D-C Circuits | 4 |
|    Resistors in Series | 4 |
|    Resistors in Parallel | 4 |
|    R-L Circuit Time Constant | 5 |
|    R-C Circuit Time Constant | 5 |
|    Comparison of Units in Electric and Magnetic Circuits | 5 |
|    Capacitors in Series | 5 |
|    Capacitors in Parallel | 5 |
|    Capacitive Reactance | 5 |
|    Impedance in an R-C Circuit (Series) | 5 |
|    Inductors in Series | 5 |
|    Inductors in Parallel | 5 |
|    Inductive Reactance | 5 |
|    Q of a Coil | 5 |
|    Impedance of an R-L Circuit (Series) | 5 |
|    Impedance with R, C, and L in Series | 5 |
|    Parallel Circuit Impedance | 5 |
|    Sine-Wave Voltage Relationships | 5 |
|    Power in A-C Circuit | 6 |
|    Transformers | 6 |
|    Three-Phase Voltage and Current Relationships | 6 |
| **GREEK ALPHABET** | 7 |
|    Alpha ...... Omega | 7 |
| **COMMON ABBREVIATIONS AND LETTER SYMBOLS** | 8 |
|    Alternating Current (noun) ...... Watt | 8 |

# ELECTRICAL TERMS AND FORMULAS

## Terms

AGONIC.—An imaginary line of the earth's surface passing through points where the magnetic declination is 0°; that is, points where the compass points to true north.

AMMETER.—An instrument for measuring the amount of electron flow in amperes.

AMPERE.—The basic unit of electrical current.

AMPERE-TURN.—The magnetizing force produced by a current of one ampere flowing through a coil of one turn.

AMPLIDYNE.—A rotary magnetic or dynamoelectric amplifier used in servomechanism and control applications.

AMPLIFICATION.—The process of increasing the strength (current, power, or voltage) of a signal.

AMPLIFIER.—A device used to increase the signal voltage, current, or power, generally composed of a vacuum tube and associated circuit called a stage. It may contain several stages in order to obtain a desired gain.

AMPLITUDE.—The maximum instantaneous value of an alternating voltage or current, measured in either the positive or negative direction.

ARC.—A flash caused by an electric current ionizing a gas or vapor.

ARMATURE.—The rotating part of an electric motor or generator. The moving part of a relay or vibrator.

ATTENUATOR.—A network of resistors used to reduce voltage, current, or power delivered to a load.

AUTOTRANSFORMER.—A transformer in which the primary and secondary are connected together in one winding.

BATTERY.—Two or more primary or secondary cells connected together electrically. The term does not apply to a single cell.

BREAKER POINTS.—Metal contacts that open and close a circuit at timed intervals.

BRIDGE CIRCUIT.—The electrical bridge circuit is a term referring to any one of a variety of electric circuit networks, one branch of which, the "bridge" proper, connects two points of equal potential and hence carries no current when the circuit is properly adjusted or balanced.

BRUSH.—The conducting material, usually a block of carbon, bearing against the commutator or sliprings through which the current flows in or out.

BUS BAR.—A primary power distribution point connected to the main power source.

CAPACITOR.—Two electrodes or sets of electrodes in the form of plates, separated from each other by an insulating material called the dielectric.

CHOKE COIL.—A coil of low ohmic resistance and high impedance to alternating current.

CIRCUIT.—The complete path of an electric current.

CIRCUIT BREAKER.—An electromagnetic or thermal device that opens a circuit when the current in the circuit exceeds a predetermined amount. Circuit breakers can be reset.

CIRCULAR MIL.—An area equal to that of a circle with a diameter of 0.001 inch. It is used for measuring the cross section of wires.

COAXIAL CABLE.—A transmission line consisting of two conductors concentric with and insulated from each other.

COMMUTATOR.—The copper segments on the armature of a motor or generator. It is cylindrical in shape and is used to pass power into or from the brushes. It is a switching device.

CONDUCTANCE.—The ability of a material to conduct or carry an electric current. It is the reciprocal of the resistance of the material, and is expressed in mhos.

CONDUCTIVITY.—The ease with which a substance transmits electricity.

CONDUCTOR.—Any material suitable for carrying electric current.

CORE.—A magnetic material that affords an easy path for magnetic flux lines in a coil.

COUNTER E.M.F.—Counter electromotive force; an e.m.f. induced in a coil or armature that opposes the applied voltage.

CURRENT LIMITER.—A protective device similar to a fuse, usually used in high amperage circuits.

CYCLE.—One complete positive and one complete negative alternation of a current or voltage.

DIELECTRIC.—An insulator; a term that refers to the insulating material between the plates of a capacitor.

## ELECTRICAL TERMS AND FORMULAS

**DIODE.**—Vacuum tube—a two element tube that contains a cathode and plate; semiconductor—a material of either germanium or silicon that is manufactured to allow current to flow in only one direction. Diodes are used as rectifiers and detectors.

**DIRECT CURRENT.**—An electric current that flows in one direction only.

**EDDY CURRENT.**—Induced circulating currents in a conducting material that are caused by a varying magnetic field.

**EFFICIENCY.**—The ratio of output power to input power, generally expressed as a percentage.

**ELECTROLYTE.**—A solution of a substance which is capable of conducting electricity. An electrolyte may be in the form of either a liquid or a paste.

**ELECTROMAGNET.**—A magnet made by passing current through a coil of wire wound on a soft iron core.

**ELECTROMOTIVE FORCE (e.m.f.).**—The force that produces an electric current in a circuit.

**ELECTRON.**—A negatively charged particle of matter.

**ENERGY.**—The ability or capacity to do work.

**FARAD.**—The unit of capacitance.

**FEEDBACK.**—A transfer of energy from the output circuit of a device back to its input.

**FIELD.**—The space containing electric or magnetic lines of force.

**FIELD WINDING.**—The coil used to provide the magnetizing force in motors and generators.

**FLUX FIELD.**—All electric or magnetic lines of force in a given region.

**FREE ELECTRONS.**—Electrons which are loosely held and consequently tend to move at random among the atoms of the material.

**FREQUENCY.**—The number of complete cycles per second existing in any form of wave motion; such as the number of cycles per second of an alternating current.

**FULL-WAVE RECTIFIER CIRCUIT.**—A circuit which utilizes both the positive and the negative alternations of an alternating current to produce a direct current.

**FUSE.**—A protective device inserted in series with a circuit. It contains a metal that will melt or break when current is increased beyond a specific value for a definite period of time.

**GAIN.**—The ratio of the output power, voltage, or current to the input power, voltage, or current, respectively.

**GALVANOMETER.**—An instrument used to measure small d-c currents.

**GENERATOR.**—A machine that converts mechanical energy into electrical energy.

**GROUND.**—A metallic connection with the earth to establish ground potential. Also, a common return to a point of zero potential. The chassis of a receiver or a transmitter is sometimes the common return, and therefore the ground of the unit.

**HENRY.**—The basic unit of inductance.

**HORSEPOWER.**—The English unit of power, equal to work done at the rate of 550 foot-pounds per second. Equal to 746 watts of electrical power.

**HYSTERESIS.**—A lagging of the magnetic flux in a magnetic material behind the magnetizing force which is producing it.

**IMPEDANCE.**—The total opposition offered to the flow of an alternating current. It may consist of any combination of resistance, inductive reactance, and capacitive reactance.

**INDUCTANCE.**—The property of a circuit which tends to oppose a change in the existing current.

**INDUCTION.**—The act or process of producing voltage by the relative motion of a magnetic field across a conductor.

**INDUCTIVE REACTANCE.**—The opposition to the flow of alternating or pulsating current caused by the inductance of a circuit. It is measured in ohms.

**INPHASE.**—Applied to the condition that exists when two waves of the same frequency pass through their maximum and minimum values of like polarity at the same instant.

**INVERSELY.**—Inverted or reversed in position or relationship.

**ISOGONIC LINE.**—An imaginary line drawn through points on the earth's surface where the magnetic deviation is equal.

**JOULE.**—A unit of energy or work. A joule of energy is liberated by one ampere flowing for one second through a resistance of one ohm.

**KILO.**—A prefix meaning 1,000.

**LAG.**—The amount one wave is behind another in time; expressed in electrical degrees.

**LAMINATED CORE.**—A core built up from thin sheets of metal and used in transformers and relays.

**LEAD.**—The opposite of LAG. Also, a wire or connection.

## ELECTRICAL TERMS AND FORMULAS

LINE OF FORCE.—A line in an electric or magnetic field that shows the direction of the force.

LOAD.—The power that is being delivered by any power producing device. The equipment that uses the power from the power producing device.

MAGNETIC AMPLIFIER.—A saturable reactor type device that is used in a circuit to amplify or control.

MAGNETIC CIRCUIT.—The complete path of magnetic lines of force.

MAGNETIC FIELD.—The space in which a magnetic force exists.

MAGNETIC FLUX.—The total number of lines of force issuing from a pole of a magnet.

MAGNETIZE.—To convert a material into a magnet by causing the molecules to rearrange.

MAGNETO.—A generator which produces alternating current and has a permanent magnet as its field.

MEGGER.—A test instrument used to measure insulation resistance and other high resistances. It is a portable hand operated d-c generator used as an ohmmeter.

MEGOHM.—A million ohms.

MICRO.—A prefix meaning one-millionth.

MILLI.—A prefix meaning one-thousandth.

MILLIAMMETER.—An ammeter that measures current in thousandths of an ampere.

MOTOR-GENERATOR.—A motor and a generator with a common shaft used to convert line voltages to other voltages or frequencies.

MUTUAL INDUCTANCE.—A circuit property existing when the relative position of two inductors causes the magnetic lines of force from one to link with the turns of the other.

NEGATIVE CHARGE.—The electrical charge carried by a body which has an excess of electrons.

NEUTRON.—A particle having the weight of a proton but carrying no electric charge. It is located in the nucleus of an atom.

NUCLEUS.—The central part of an atom that is mainly comprised of protons and neutrons. It is the part of the atom that has the most mass.

NULL.—Zero.

OHM.—The unit of electrical resistance.

OHMMETER.—An instrument for directly measuring resistance in ohms.

OVERLOAD.—A load greater than the rated load of an electrical device.

PERMALLOY.—An alloy of nickel and iron having an abnormally high magnetic permeability.

PERMEABILITY.—A measure of the ease with which magnetic lines of force can flow through a material as compared to air.

PHASE DIFFERENCE.—The time in electrical degrees by which one wave leads or lags another.

POLARITY.—The character of having magnetic poles, or electric charges.

POLE.—The section of a magnet where the flux lines are concentrated; also where they enter and leave the magnet. An electrode of a battery.

POLYPHASE.—A circuit that utilizes more than one phase of alternating current.

POSITIVE CHARGE.—The electrical charge carried by a body which has become deficient in electrons.

POTENTIAL.—The amount of charge held by a body as compared to another point or body. Usually measured in volts.

POTENTIOMETER.—A variable voltage divider; a resistor which has a variable contact arm so that any portion of the potential applied between its ends may be selected.

POWER.—The rate of doing work or the rate of expending energy. The unit of electrical power is the watt.

POWER FACTOR.—The ratio of the actual power of an alternating or pulsating current, as measured by a wattmeter, to the apparent power, as indicated by ammeter and voltmeter readings. The power factor of an inductor, capacitor, or insulator is an expression of their losses.

PRIME MOVER.—The source of mechanical power used to drive the rotor of a generator.

PROTON.—A positively charged particle in the nucleus of an atom.

RATIO.—The value obtained by dividing one number by another, indicating their relative proportions.

REACTANCE.—The opposition offered to the flow of an alternating current by the inductance, capacitance, or both, in any circuit.

RECTIFIERS.—Devices used to change alternating current to unidirectional current. These may be vacuum tubes, semiconductors such as germanium and silicon, and dry-disk rectifiers such as selenium and copper-oxide.

RELAY.—An electromechanical switching device that can be used as a remote control.

RELUCTANCE.—A measure of the opposition that a material offers to magnetic lines of force.

RESISTANCE.—The opposition to the flow of current caused by the nature and physical dimensions of a conductor.

RESISTOR.—A circuit element whose chief characteristic is resistance; used to oppose the flow of current.

## ELECTRICAL TERMS AND FORMULAS

RETENTIVITY.—The measure of the ability of a material to hold its magnetism.

RHEOSTAT.—A variable resistor.

SATURABLE REACTOR.—A control device that uses a small d-c current to control a large a-c current by controlling core flux density.

SATURATION.—The condition existing in any circuit when an increase in the driving signal produces no further change in the resultant effect.

SELF-INDUCTION.—The process by which a circuit induces an e.m.f. into itself by its own magnetic field.

SERIES-WOUND.—A motor or generator in which the armature is wired in series with the field winding.

SERVO.—A device used to convert a small movement into one of greater movement or force.

SERVOMECHANISM.—A closed-loop system that produces a force to position an object in accordance with the information that originates at the input.

SOLENOID.—An electromagnetic coil that contains a movable plunger.

SPACE CHARGE.—The cloud of electrons existing in the space between the cathode and plate in a vacuum tube, formed by the electrons emitted from the cathode in excess of those immediately attracted to the plate.

SPECIFIC GRAVITY—The ratio between the density of a substance and that of pure water, at a given temperature.

SYNCHROSCOPE—An instrument used to indicate a difference in frequency between two a-c sources.

SYNCHRO SYSTEM.—An electrical system that gives remote indications or control by means of self-synchronizing motors.

TACHOMETER.—An instrument for indicating revolutions per minute.

TERTIARY WINDING.—A third winding on a transformer or magnetic amplifier that is used as a second control winding.

THERMISTOR.—A resistor that is used to compensate for temperature variations in a circuit.

THERMOCOUPLE.—A junction of two dissimilar metals that produces a voltage when heated.

TORQUE.—The turning effort or twist which a shaft sustains when transmitting power.

TRANSFORMER.—A device composed of two or more coils, linked by magnetic lines of force, used to transfer energy from one circuit to another.

TRANSMISSION LINES.—Any conductor or system of conductors used to carry electrical energy from its source to a load.

VARS.—Abbreviation for volt-ampere, reactive.

VECTOR.—A line used to represent both direction and magnitude.

VOLT.—The unit of electrical potential.

VOLTMETER.—An instrument designed to measure a difference in electrical potential, in volts.

WATT.—The unit of electrical power.

WATTMETER.—An instrument for measuring electrical power in watts.

# Formulas

Ohm's Law for d-c Circuits

$$I = \frac{E}{R} = \frac{P}{E} = \sqrt{\frac{P}{R}}$$

$$R = \frac{E}{I} = \frac{P}{I^2} = \frac{E^2}{P}$$

$$E = IR = \frac{P}{I} = \sqrt{PR}$$

$$P = EI = \frac{E^2}{R} = I^2 R$$

Resistors in Series

$$R_T = R_1 + R_2 \ldots$$

Resistors in Parallel
Two resistors

$$R_T = \frac{R_1 R_2}{R_1 + R_2}$$

More than two

$$\frac{1}{R_T} = \frac{1}{R_1} + \frac{1}{R_2} + \frac{1}{R_3}$$

# ELECTRICAL TERMS AND FORMULAS

R-L Circuit Time Constant equals

$$\frac{L \text{ (in henrys)}}{R \text{ (in ohms)}} = t \text{ (in seconds), or}$$

$$\frac{L \text{ (in microhenrys)}}{R \text{ (in ohms)}} = t \text{ (in microseconds)}$$

R-C Circuit Time Constant equals
R (ohms) X C (farads) = t (seconds)
R (megohms) x C (microfarads) = t (seconds)
R (ohms) x C (microfarads) = t (microseconds)
R (megohms) x C (micromicrofrads) = t (microseconds)

### Comparison of Units in Electric and Magnetic Circuits.

|  | Electric circuit | Magnetic circuit |
|---|---|---|
| Force | Volt, E or e.m.f. | Gilberts, F, or m.m.f. |
| Flow | Ampere, I | Flux, $\Phi$, in maxwells |
| Opposition | Ohms, R | Reluctance, R |
| Law | Ohm's law, $I = \frac{E}{R}$ | Rowland's law $\Phi = \frac{F}{R}$ |
| Intensity of force | Volts per cm. of length | $H = \frac{1.257 IN}{L}$, gilberts per centimeter of length |
| Density | Current density— for example, amperes per $cm^2$. | Flux density—for example, lines per $cm^2$., or gausses |

**Capacitors in Series**
Two capacitors

$$C_T = \frac{C_1 C_2}{C_1 + C_2}$$

More than two

$$\frac{1}{C_T} = \frac{1}{C_1} + \frac{1}{C_2} + \frac{1}{C_3} \cdots$$

**Capacitors in Parallel**

$$C_T = C_1 + C_2 \cdots$$

**Capacitive Reactance**

$$X_c = \frac{1}{2\pi f C}$$

**Impedance in an R-C Circuit (Series)**

$$Z = \sqrt{R^2 + X_c^2}$$

**Inductors in Series**

$$L_T = L_1 + L_2 \ldots \text{(No coupling between coils)}$$

**Inductors in Parallel**
Two inductors

$$L_T = \frac{L_1 L_2}{L_1 + L_2} \text{(No coupling between coils)}$$

More than two

$$\frac{1}{L_T} = \frac{1}{L_1} + \frac{1}{L_2} + \frac{1}{L_3} \ldots \text{(No coupling between coils)}$$

**Inductive Reactance**

$$X_L = 2\pi f L$$

**Q of a Coil**

$$Q = \frac{X_L}{R}$$

**Impedance of an R-L Circuit (series)**

$$Z = \sqrt{R^2 + X_L^2}$$

**Impedance with R, C, and L in Series**

$$Z = \sqrt{R^2 + (X_L - X_C)^2}$$

**Parallel Circuit Impedance**

$$Z = \frac{Z_1 Z_2}{Z_1 + Z_2}$$

**Sine-Wave Voltage Relationships**
Average value

$$E_{ave} = \frac{2}{\pi} \times E_{max} = 0.637 E_{max}$$

## ELECTRICAL TERMS AND FORMULAS

Effective or r.m.s. value

$$E_{eff} = \frac{E_{max}}{\sqrt{2}} = \frac{E_{max}}{1.414} = 0.707 E_{max} = 1.11 E_{ave}$$

Maximum value

$$E_{max} = \sqrt{2} E_{eff} = 1.414 E_{eff} = 1.57 E_{ave}$$

Voltage in an a-c circuit

$$E = IZ = \frac{P}{I \times P.F.}$$

Current in an a-c circuit

$$I = \frac{E}{Z} = \frac{P}{E \times P.F.}$$

Power in A-C Circuit
Apparent power = $EI$
True power

$$P = EI \cos \theta = EI \times P.F.$$

Power factor

$$P.F. = \frac{P}{EI} = \cos \theta$$

$$\cos \theta = \frac{\text{true power}}{\text{apparent power}}$$

Transformers
Voltage relationship

$$\frac{E}{E} = \frac{N}{N} \quad \text{or} \quad E = E \times \frac{N}{N}$$

Current relationship

$$\frac{I_p}{I_s} = \frac{N_s}{N_p}$$

Induced voltage

$$E_{eff} = 4.44 \, BAfN \cdot 10^{-8}$$

Turns ratio equals

$$\frac{N_p}{N_s} = \sqrt{\frac{Z_p}{Z_s}}$$

Secondary current

$$I_s = I_p \frac{N_p}{N_s}$$

Secondary voltage

$$E_s = E_p \frac{N_s}{N_p}$$

Three Phase Voltage and Current Relationships
With wye connected windings

$$E_{line} = 1.732 E_{coil} = \sqrt{3} E_{coil}$$

$$I_{line} = I_{coil}$$

With delta connected windings

$$E_{line} = E_{coil}$$

$$I_{line} = 1.732 I_{coil}$$

With wye or delta connected winding

$$P_{coil} = E_{coil} I_{coil}$$

$$P_t = 3 P_{coil}$$

$$P_t = 1.732 E_{line} I_{line}$$

(To convert to true power multiply by $\cos \theta$)

Synchronous Speed of Motor

$$\text{r.p.m.} = \frac{120 \times \text{frequency}}{\text{number of poles}}$$

# GREEK ALPHABET

| Name | Capital | Lower Case | Designates |
|---|---|---|---|
| Alpha | A | $\alpha$ | Angles. |
| Beta | B | $\beta$ | Angles, flux density. |
| Gamma | $\Gamma$ | $\gamma$ | Conductivity. |
| Delta | $\Delta$ | $\delta$ | Variation of a quantity, increment. |
| Epsilon | E | $\epsilon$ | Base of natural logarithms (2.71828). |
| Zeta | Z | $\zeta$ | Impedance, coefficients, coordinates. |
| Eta | H | $\eta$ | Hysteresis coefficient, efficiency, magnetizing force. |
| Theta | $\Theta$ | $\theta$ | Phase angle. |
| Iota | I | $\iota$ | |
| Kappa | K | $\kappa$ | Dielectric constant, coupling coefficient, susceptibility. |
| Lambda | $\Lambda$ | $\lambda$ | Wavelength. |
| Mu | M | $\mu$ | Permeability, micro, amplification factor. |
| Nu | N | $\nu$ | Reluctivity. |
| Xi | $\Xi$ | $\xi$ | |
| Omicron | O | o | |
| Pi | $\Pi$ | $\pi$ | 3.1416 |
| Rho | P | $\rho$ | Resistivity. |
| Sigma | $\Sigma$ | $\sigma$ | |
| Tau | T | $\tau$ | Time constant, time-phase displacement. |
| Upsilon | $\Upsilon$ | $\upsilon$ | |
| Phi | $\Phi$ | $\varphi$ | Angles, magnetic flux. |
| Chi | X | $\chi$ | |
| Psi | $\Psi$ | $\psi$ | Dielectric flux, phase difference. |
| Omega | $\Omega$ | $\omega$ | Ohms (capital), angular velocity ($2\pi f$). |

# COMMON ABBREVIATIONS AND LETTER SYMBOLS

| Term | Abbreviation or Symbol |
|---|---|
| alternating current (noun) | a.c. |
| alternating-current (adj.) | a-c |
| ampere | a. |
| area | A |
| audiofrequency (noun) | AF |
| audiofrequency (adj.) | A-F |
| capacitance | C |
| capacitive reactance | $X_C$ |
| centimeter | cm. |
| conductance | G |
| coulomb | Q |
| counterelectromotive force | c.e.m.f. |
| current (d-c or r.m.s. value) | I |
| current (instantaneous value) | i |
| cycles per second | c.p.s. |
| dielectric constant | K,k |
| difference in potential (d-c or r.m.s. value) | E |
| difference in potential (instantaneous value) | e |
| direct current (noun) | d.c. |
| direct-current (adj.) | d-c |
| electromotive force | e.m.f. |
| frequency | f |
| henry | h. |
| horsepower | hp. |
| impedance | Z |
| inductance | L |
| inductive reactance | $X_L$ |
| kilovolt | kv. |
| kilovolt-ampere | kv.-a. |
| kilowatt | kw. |
| kilowatt-hour | kw.-hr. |
| magnetic field intensity | H |
| magnetomotive force | m.m.f. |
| megohm | M |
| microampere | $\mu$a. |
| microfarad | $\mu$f. |
| microhenry | $\mu$h. |
| micromicrofarad | $\mu\mu$f. |
| microvolt | $\mu$v. |
| milliampere | ma. |
| millihenry | mh. |
| milliwatt | mw. |
| mutual inductance | M |
| power | P |
| resistance | R |
| revolutions per minute | r.p.m. |
| root mean square | r.m.s. |
| time | t |
| torque | T |
| volt | v. |
| watt | w. |

www.ingramcontent.com/pod-product-compliance
Lightning Source LLC
Chambersburg PA
CBHW082210300426
44117CB00016B/2741